Enc

Antagonistic polemics are often characterized by labeling one's opponent with the most extreme example of those who hold similar views as the opponent. Broad-brush polemics are the favorite tool of every crusading demagogue and pulpiteer who tries to build a following at someone else's expense. Just like Goldilocks had to work to find porridge that was neither too hot nor too cold, but just right, sometimes finding a perspective on a topic that is "just right" can be equally challenging in an emotionally charged polemic atmosphere.

The topic of glossolalia, which is "speaking in tongues," has been just such a polarizing topic for over a century. It has been the victim of some very broad-brush polemics and overgeneralizations from both the "pro" and "anti" camps. The pull to the extremes of demeaning neglect and outright denunciation on the one hand, or an overemphasis and overvaluation on the other, are nearly irresistible. It is hard to find porridge that is just right.

In this work Steve Bremner addresses several of the worn-out myths, canards, and misrepresentations concerning the gift of tongues. Steve is unapologetic about his Pentecostal heritage in both theology and personal experience. In an easily readable style, Steve advocates for the spiritual value of speaking in other tongues while avoiding making it a metric for an alleged level of advanced spirituality—a chronic problem in many traditional Pentecostal environments. This book is not rigorously theological and academics might find fault with it. However, for those who are looking for a "reachable" primer on the topic from a "pro" perspective, I recommend this work from my good friend Steve Bremner.

DR. STEPHEN R. CROSBY
Stephanos Ministries
Monroe, NC
www.stevecrosby.org
www.stevecrosby.com

In a day of much ignorance, misunderstanding, and controversy regarding the Pentecostal phenomena of speaking in tongues, Steve Bremner does the body of Christ a great service in dealing with the lies that hinder many from receiving and functioning in this sacred heavenly language. The basic tendency of human nature is to reject what we don't understand. Give this book a chance and allow it to open the eyes of your understanding and shed new light on this vitally important subject.

BERT FARIAS
Holy Fire Ministries

While I haven't yet met Steve in person, we've talked and interacted online quite a bit, and I have to tell you that the guy who writes the books is the guy I talk to in real life. He writes like he lives, and he lives like he writes. He is smart, funny, approachable, and down to earth. He makes truth about God, theology, and life clear and simple, without neglecting good scholarship for the theologically minded.

This book was fun to read. I was reminded of my own life several times while reading it—transitioning from a non-Pentecostal/charismatic denomination (Baptist, in my case; Plymouth Brethren in his) to a charismatic nondenominational stream, interacting with friends from both types of backgrounds over the years, making some of the mistakes Steve's friends made in his story, watching my life and others' lives get impacted as a result of this gift, and getting to help lots of people receive this aspect of the Holy Spirit's ministry by walking them through the same truths found here.

In this book, Steve overcomes the most common difficulties people have with speaking in tongues by explaining the relevant Scriptures simply and to the point, with dashes of humor and his own life story thrown in for good measure. So if you want to learn more about speaking in tongues—whether or not you believe it's for you—then this book is a good place to start. If you already believe but have had some type of difficulty receiving, this is also a great book to help you overcome the more common hindrances people run into. Get ready to receive this gift like we do every good thing God gives—by grace through faith.

Great job, Steve! Keep 'em coming!

Joshua Greeson
Author of *God's Will Is Always Healing*

Okay. I understand. Speaking in tongues is spooky to you or you think it's way too weird for your taste. At the same time, something tells you that there has to be "something" to it. Steve Bremner's book will help you ease into the solid truth of what speaking in tongues is all about. He is not forceful in his delivery, just informative, lovingly so. You'll be glad you read this book, even if for informative purposes. It's an easy read and will not bore you. Even if you already speak in tongues, this book will help you understand some points of interest you may not have thought about previously. It also gives you great pointers to share when those who don't understand why people speak in tongues approach you. Enjoy the read while increasing your knowledge for life.

Dr. Shane Wall

Author of *Understanding*

Speaking in tongues is not as weird as you think. Steve beautifully removes fear that hinders many from enjoying one of the most beautiful gifts given from God, by clearly articulating his experience in a refreshing and relatable teaching.

Jeremy Mangerchine

Author *of The Longest Bridge Across Water*

Jesus prophesied in Mark 16:17 that all those who believe in him will speak in other tongues. Only a few days after he uttered those words, his promise was fulfilled. In Acts 2:1-4 we see God's prototype church—the first of its kind—and 100 percent of them "began to speak in other tongues as the Spirit enabled them" (NIV). No one was excluded. But due to well-meaning, confused people in the body of Christ throughout the centuries, many lies have developed about this gift from God (most or all of them in the last century alone).

Thankfully, God sent another gift to the church—a guy named Steve Bremner—who has masterfully tackled the most common lies people believe with tact, whit, Scripture, and sensibility. If you've ever had questions about speaking in tongues, or if you've ever been challenged about your beliefs, this book is sure to give you the confidence you need to move forward in your faith and even lead others into the experience we call the baptism in the Holy Spirit.

Art Thomas

Missionary-Evangelist and CEO of

Wildfire Ministries International

It's not easy to take on a complex and controversial subject like speaking in tongues. Steve has shown great courage in tackling this spirited issue and has done so in a way that encourages us instead of making us feel judged or condemned. Steve exposes some critical misconceptions that many of us don't even know we have but should be thrilled to pull out of our theology. His goal is clear in his desire to help us move closer to Jesus and enjoy the gifts he's made available to us. This is an important work and my understanding has grown because of it.

JESSE BIRKEY
Author *of Life Resurrected: Extraordinary Miracles through Ordinary People*

The view that supernatural Christianity has passed away subconsciously suggests that God gave better gifts to the saints in the Bible than he gives to us today: "Sorry, I see you need help, but I only helped those who lived when I was constructing the Bible." We would never imagine God saying something like this to his people, but this is exactly what cessationism implies. Our God is supernatural and he loves us just as much today as he loved the disciples on the day he poured his Spirit out on them. They began to speak in languages they had never learned before. This was a statement that God would transcend communication so that his power and love could fill the earth. Speaking in tongues is essential to the expansion of the kingdom of God. It is a key foundation gift for every believer.

Steve Bremner is a man who embodies this gift. He writes from his life, and shares in this book a much-needed paradigm for the understanding and activation of this gift.

DAVE EDWARDS
Revival Pastor, Bethel Atlanta School of Supernatural Ministry
Author of *Activating a Prophetic Lifestyle*

John & Joanne

I hope all is well with you and your family, and that by the time you get this you will have had a wonderful Christmas holiday.

Included is a copy of my first traditionally published book with a personalized touch, as well as a copy for Scot & Jeanie. I would be grateful if you could pass a copy of it on to them as a thanks for all they do for us missionaries on the field so we can be fruitful for the kingdom.
Here's hoping you have a fruitful and blessed 2016.

Blessings and fire on your heads,

Steve, Lili and Jemina Bremner

John & Joanne

NINE LIES
PEOPLE BELIEVE ABOUT
Speaking
IN
Tongues

Thank you for being friends
and mentors over the years &
encouraging my writing & podcasting
from the mission field.
Lili & I appreciate you more
than words can say.
Blessings & fire on your head,

NINE LIES
PEOPLE BELIEVE ABOUT

Speaking
IN
Tongues

STEVE BREMNER

DESTINY IMAGE® PUBLISHERS, INC.
P.O. Box 310, Shippensburg, PA 17257-0310
"Promoting Inspired Lives."

This book and all other Destiny Image and Destiny Image Fiction books are available at Christian bookstores and distributors worldwide.

Cover design by Eileen Rockwell

For more information on foreign distributors, call 717-532-3040.
Reach us on the Internet: www.destinyimage.com.

ISBN 13 TP: 978-0-7684-0851-5
ISBN 13 eBook: 978-0-7684-0852-2

For Worldwide Distribution, Printed in the U.S.A.
1 2 3 4 5 6 7 8 / 20 19 18 17 16

Acknowledgments

I felt it would be inappropriate not to include a moment to give thanks to the many friends and volunteers who helped make this book what it is today. As such, I will not be able to thank every single individual who could be thanked for this project coming together, and I hope I don't offend anybody I unintentionally left out. There are simply too many to list and personally thank.

In writing a book about speaking in tongues, it would be criminal of me not to personally thank Brian Parkman for all the seeds you planted in my spirit on this subject in both Bible college and in calls over the years. Much of what I've taught others and what I've written in this book would never have come about if not for your influence. Thank you for being available over Skype at random times of the day to let me pick your brain about this subject. I am especially thankful for your contribution in the form of cowriting a chapter and letting me use your class handout as an appendix in this book.

I also thank Joel Crumpton, not only for teaching me a lot about this subject as well, but for answering my questions and giving me your opinions when I've wanted to pick your brain, as well as the ways you've been willing to teach through hands-on training on the streets of Charlotte, North Carolina. I owe much of what I believe and live out to you and Brian, two great men of

God. Only the Lord knows how many people have been baptized in the Holy Spirit and spoken in tongues through my ministry in a way that is directly attributable to you both.

To Dr. Stephen Crosby, for not only being willing to come on my podcast many times and share your expertise and tweetable quotes, but for being willing to take a look at my mess of a manuscript and provide invaluable insights that ultimately have strengthened this work and given it more depth and breadth. The result is more theological oomph when and where that was most needed.

I certainly don't want to forget to thank Roy Farias for the tremendous editing he did on this project. You have helped take this book to another level I only dreamed possible. Every author needs a Roy Farias! And I also want to thank those of you who've encouraged my writing gift and made me think "why not?" when it comes to publishing a work such as this.

Of course, I've had many volunteers and personal friends proofread and review the manuscript in various stages, and to each of you I'm eternally grateful. I want to thank Royce Tyler for being the first to respond and get back to me with constructive feedback when I announced on social media that I was looking for proofreaders. I told you I'd mention you in my next book. I want to thank Kathryn Hughey for always being a helping hand in editing my work, and helping me understand the bizarre world of commas. I want to thank Seth Roach for always encouraging me in my writings, my podcast, and for having incredibly timely words. You have been an example to me of what can happen when believers put into practice things the Spirit showed them through this book. I'm grateful to know you. I especially want to thank Brad Herman for believing in this book. I also want to thank the team at Destiny Image for taking this book and doing your magic with it.

And I want to thank my wife, Lili, for not only being willing to be my wife, but for giving me space on some occasions when the anointing just "came on me" in writing this and I needed to be left to work. God has given you a lot of patience and encouragement, and I'm extremely happy to have you and Jemina along for the journey.

Finally, I obviously don't want to leave out my Lord and Savior, Jesus Christ. I owe you everything.

Contents

Preface

*S*ome authors affectionately refer to their books as their babies, which becomes especially relevant to me and this work. At the time of writing this preface, I have one daughter, an incredibly hilarious toddler named Jemina. We almost thought she was going to come into the world two days sooner than she actually did.

We had gone to see our doctor for what we thought was going to be a routine checkup one Monday morning and to make sure a concern Lili had was nothing to be alarmed about. Our doctor was on vacation, as it was still over two weeks before the expected delivery date, so we ended up seeing another doctor. The doctor we spoke with in his place encouraged us to begin the protocols they follow to prepare for a Cesarean section. This was not so good, as we were not prepared for anything other than a natural delivery, and if we were to have Jemina that day, we would especially not have been ready financially. This particular doctor was not even willing to try a natural delivery, but wanted to proceed with a C-section.

I pretended that I spoke very little Spanish (cuando en realidad hablo más que adecuada Español), and we called our friend and leader Anna Burgess to come to the hospital to translate for me. Really we just wanted someone else who had navigated the confusing world of Peruvian hospitals and births to help bring us some peace by her presence. I went to the closest ATM I could find and withdrew all the cash I had in any of our bank accounts in order to pay for the bill, believing by faith that Lili would deliver Jemina naturally and without having to have her stomach cut open.

By lunchtime, we were worn out and felt like we had just been through a few days of stress and uncertainty as opposed to merely a few hours. Lili was not dilated enough to give birth, and I thought this doctor really wanted to make his money off of us and perform a C-section. Amidst all of the confusion and the seeming pressure that this was when we were going to bring our first daughter into the world, the three of us took a moment to pray and listen to the still small voice of the Holy Spirit. We then collectively sensed that now was not the time, and Lili and I were not to bow to any pressure from a doctor we had only met that morning. Lili got herself dressed and we decided to take a taxi and head to another hospital for a second opinion, this time opting to go where Anna had delivered her youngest son just a few years prior.

First we needed to eat since Lili hadn't had anything to eat since early that morning, and if this second hospital decided Lili couldn't have a natural delivery but was going to give birth that afternoon, then we knew she would have been out of energy if she had essentially fasted all day. As we sat down at a Chifa restaurant (the Peruvian version of Chinese food, which you have got to try, by the way), Anna lent me her iPhone so I could check my e-mail and Facebook messages. That's when I read a note from a friend.

In his message, which I'm paraphrasing here, he told us that in the last couple of weeks leading up to the delivery, Lili would feel contractions and that she was not to worry, but that it was best we wait until heading to the hospital. Since we were first-time parents we might not know that Lili could have contractions for days before giving birth, and we may be tempted to go into the hospital early, at which point they follow their protocols and the chances of a probable C-section are increased. He told us he felt led to write that message and tell us that when Lili is ready to give birth, *she will know it* and not need a doctor to convince her.

I quickly wrote back indicating we received his message as confirmation from the Lord as we were just in that whirlwind situation and had almost caved in to the pressure the doctor was putting on us. Later when we were home and had Internet access again, I wrote this friend back and told him in more detail what had happened, and why his message was timely for us.

This was his response:

> I just wanted to let you know I completed the book and thoroughly enjoyed it. I am really encouraged to pray in the Spirit more and will be checking out some of the resources in the back of the book. Interesting thing is the day I sent you that Facebook message, I had just spent some of my lunchtime in my car at the park praying in tongues, and when I was done the encouragement to wait about the delivery came to me at the end of it. I didn't really even think it was a word from the Lord or anything but it was strong

on my heart and felt like writing it. So I was deeply encouraged as well by it.

This encouraged me—obviously. You see, this man had just finished reading an advanced preview copy of the book you're now reading. This was the first of many testimonies I started hearing from people after having read it for themselves. This past year has been just a taste of the Lord's impact of this book on the bride of Christ.

We wound up meeting the doctor who was to deliver Jemina into the world two days later on Wednesday night. We still had a C-section, in case you're wondering, but this doctor was willing to go the natural route first. After two hours of labor and Lili not being able to take it any more, we were comfortable going forward with the surgery. I mention this because having had two more days gave us enough time to launch a Go Fund Me campaign and ask the body of Christ for help in our situation, and we were blessed and humbled by the abundant financial help people offered.

Exactly two weeks later, on my daughter's original expected due date, I self-published this book on Amazon.

STEVE BREMNER
April 3, 2015

Why I Wrote This Book

Whven I started writing *Nine Lies People Believe About Speaking in Tongues* about a year earlier, I didn't believe there were very many "fresh revelation" books on the power of speaking in tongues out there besides Dave Roberson's *The Walk of the Spirit, The Walk of Power: The Vital Role of Praying in Tongues.* Although I could have developed this book to fill that void, I don't presume to think of myself in the same league as men like my friend Brian Parkman who introduced me to Roberson, both of whom have spent decades praying in tongues daily—men who have been doing this longer than I've even been alive.

I've read many books that have come my way and I've received a few powerful nuggets here and there, but I'm convinced there's very little else out there like Roberson's book, which, at the time he wrote it, was born out of twenty-five years of daily praying in tongues. I also realize I could write a much better book in my fifties or sixties than I could now because I'm always improving in my writing gift over time. But I'm burning to stir as many people up as possible to this wonderful gift and not waste any time in not exercising it on a daily basis.

Every time I would sit down to write and spend days or afternoons working on the book, I'd get hung up and procrastinate since I felt like in order to make some point more effectively I'd have to go into more of a theological angle. That was not preferable to me because this book was intended to be conversational and accessible, as well as half the length it turned out to be. *Nine Lies* is not intended to be a high-level academic book, though I've consulted such books to get my facts straight as best as I could. I've written to some men of God who are more knowledgeable with New Testament Greek than I am and asked their critical feedback to help me keep this book accurate to the Scriptures while not betraying the conversational approach I wanted it to have.

This book stayed on hiatus for a number of months in 2013 while I kept finding myself stuck in a bit of writer's block. That was until there was an evangelical conference that took place later that year called Strange Fire, basically attacking charismatics with broad strokes of the brush and insisting any form of the charismatic gifts are not for today. This book is *not* going to be about all of the gifts of the Holy Spirit, as I think there other better works I can point you to for that. However, one of the things I've noticed in reading Internet forum debates about this issue, as well as comments on my blog, personal e-mails I've received, and conversations I've had, is that people are convinced they're right on certain aspects of the gift of speaking in tongues, including many misconceptions I had already written down in a first draft of this book.

The Strange Fire conference and all of the Internet activity that followed it at the time helped light a fire in me to finally finish this project and present it to the body of Christ for encouragement. That and the fact that one of the number one Google searches leading people to my blog is for the phrase "tongues is the least of the gifts." In fact, the top blog posts on my personal site deal with speaking in tongues, which indicates to me that this book is *badly* needed today.

It is my hope and prayer that people who are looking for answers to their questions about glossolalia and charismata will come in contact with this book. If that is not you, would you please give someone you know a copy of it? Depending on whom you ask, you can find groups of Christians who believe you're not saved if you don't speak in tongues. At least, that's what I've heard people say, but I've honestly never encountered them for myself. You can find others who say that, yes, the gifts are for today but they are not for everybody. Others say no, they're not for today and if you encounter someone speaking in tongues today they're demon-possessed. I wish I could say I was joking and never heard that last one.

> **Jesus didn't place a time limit on them or any qualifier other than "those who believe"; nor did he say these are just some of the signs that accompany believers, but they're not for all believers or any other qualifier we like to put on them.**

Jesus said at the end of Mark's Gospel:

> *And these signs will accompany those who believe: in my name they will cast out demons; they will speak*

in new tongues; they will pick up serpents with their
hands; and if they drink any deadly poison, it will
not hurt them; they will lay their hands on the sick,
and they will recover. (Mark 16:17-18)

I notice there is not much more said here other than the obvious. If you're a believer, these things will happen in your life as you witness for the gospel. If you are newly saved and have never read the Bible before, would you not take verses like this at face value and assume they mean what they actually say? Jesus didn't say these signs would accompany only the disciples; Jesus didn't place a time limit on them or any qualifier other than "those who believe"; nor did he say these are just some of the signs that accompany believers, but they're not for all believers or any other qualifier we like to put on them.

It really is quite simple.

Among these signs that will follow believers are speaking in other tongues. Among them are physical healing miracles with people recovering when a Christian prays for them. Yet we have managed to still not quite get this simple concept right and have complicated it. There is division in the body of Christ made up of believers who don't agree on these very signs Jesus said would accompany his followers. To this the cessationist might say, "Yes, that does seem to be what Jesus said here, but earlier manuscripts of the New Testament don't include these last verses of Mark's Gospel, so we shouldn't take them too seriously or place a pin there and hang our theological hats on it." And that's a good point. Fortunately, we only need to look at Paul's letter to the Corinthians, and Luke's account of the Acts of the early apostles, to glean more information regarding these issues.

R. T. Kendall states in his recent book on the Holy Spirit:

I don't mean to be unfair, but I have long suspected that, were it not for the gift of tongues, many evangelicals (many of whom are not cessationists) would have no objection to the gifts of the Spirit. The stigma (offense) is not with regard to wisdom; who doesn't want and need wisdom? It is not with regard to having words of knowledge, the gift of faith, prophecy, discerning of spirits, the miraculous, or healing. The offense is invariably speaking in tongues. Why? As my friend Charles Carrin has put it, tongues is the only gift of the Spirit that challenges our pride. There is no stigma attached to any of the other gifts. Only tongues.[1]

And that is why I feel my book is needed today. On the one hand I want to help remove the stigma surrounding the gift of tongues, but I also want to help clarify the unfortunate misconceptions that prevent people from walking in the fullness of the dimensions this gift unlocks.

Many of the lies we're going to dismantle are actually things that have been said to me, sent to me in e-mails, or commented on social media in response to things I have publicly posted. Oh, and more importantly, they also include things that I have actually believed myself prior to receiving the baptism in the Holy Spirit on September 9, 2001. I believe spending a few years as a Christian without the gift of tongues followed by years of using the gift for personal edification has helped give me some insight that can make this book valuable to readers looking for a deeper spiritual life. It has also given me patience and understanding with seekers who don't understand why they have not received yet or who don't know "what the hindrance is."

Since the majority of the lies and misconceptions in which I'm referring to in this book are things many evangelicals believe and teach, the reader could be easily misled into thinking this is a "charismatic" or "Pentecostal" book. It would be easy to see my perspective that way since it's usually those groups and denominations who have a favorable stance regarding tongues and spiritual gifts. However, charismatics and Pentecostals are not off the hook as there are some rather silly and unbiblical things people in those camps do, which we will cover in this book.

This book is divided into three sections. The first section contains my personal testimony—or at least the parts of it that are relevant for you to understand why this book is ready to burst out of me. In the second and larger portion of this book, which is also the main portion, I will cover most of these lies. The third part will cover some of the benefits of regular tongue praying and some insights I feel would be beneficial to those who want to walk deeper in this. All three sections have my own personal stories interspersed and my humor, which I hope you won't mind, because, let's face it, there's a lot of humor to speaking in tongues and people's experiences regarding it.

So, without any further backdrop, let's get started.

Note

1.   R.T. Kendall, *Holy Fire: A Balanced, Biblical Look at the Holy Spirit's Work in Our Lives* (Charisma House), Location 927, Kindle.

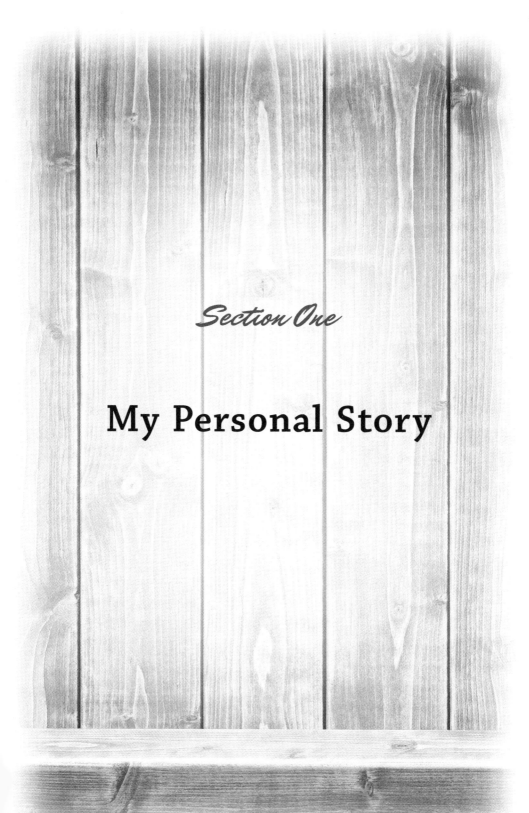

Section One

My Personal Story

Chapter 1

My Early Experience

The Beginning of an Adventure

*A*round the age of five, my family moved to the city of Peterborough, Ontario, home of music legend Stomping Tom Connors and breeding ground for many future NHL hockey players like Mike Fisher. There was a family around the corner who introduced themselves to us right away. They were Christians and nice people of whom I don't recall anything negative. Sometime when I began first grade and my little brother was old enough to walk, my mom hired a babysitter for us, named Irene, who lived further up the street. Irene, her husband, and her daughter were also Christians. Both of these families attended the same church, which happened to be within walking distance from our house and theirs.

The family who babysat my brother and me would have these weekly Bible lessons in their basement recreation room, and Doreen, the mother of the first family, would sometimes lead them, but most often it was a another lady named Diane. Every week, beginning sometime in the winter of that year, I'd go over to my babysitter's house along with other neighborhood kids, and I was exposed to the straightforward gospel.

> **I know before the Lord that I truly surrendered to him at age fifteen, at which time the adventure truly began.**

I went through Sunday school all the way up into high school. In junior high and into high school I attended youth group on most Friday nights and didn't really read the Bible all that much, but I owned a nice one. I would simply bring it to Sunday school and turn to passages that the Sunday school teachers would have us read. Other than that, it got little to no use and stayed looking brand-new for the next ten years.

Around the age of fifteen, during the late 1990s, I got serious about following God, thanks to the influence of new youth pastors who started serving at our church. It could be said that because I "prayed a prayer" one day on the way to the Bible teachings at my babysitter's house that I had accepted Christ at a young age. But I know before the Lord that I truly surrendered to him at age fifteen, at which time the adventure truly began.[1]

This youth pastor and his wife had a tremendous impact on me at the time, even if I lost touch in the next decade and remained connected mostly through social media sites. By that time in my life, however, I had been attending the same evangelical church for nearly a decade with no real commitment to Christ. I was merely dragged to church every Sunday by my parents and didn't resist too much in the process. I had not had much exposure or influence by other outside churches to even realize there was any difference between our church and any other stream of evangelicalism.

What's a "Pentecostal"?

In the eleventh grade, six months after having fully committed my life to Christ, I was actively involved in my high school's campus Christian group, which had about forty to fifty Christ followers in it. Its leadership consisted of six senior students who were about to graduate and who invited me to be one of the people to take over the group's leadership the following year. Each of the six seniors represented different denominations and church backgrounds, and I'm pretty certain this was the first time I had ever heard the word *Pentecostal*. However, at this point in time that word didn't yet mean anything to me.

By seventeen I started participating in more interdenominational events, and time and again I'd hear things about "those Pentecostals," but I still didn't think much of it at the time. Then one night we were having a slumber party at my youth pastor's house—the guys were on one floor with him, while the girls were all upstairs with his wife. I remember we somehow ended up having an informal question and answer time with him where someone asked him what the difference was between us—whatever we were—and Pentecostals. He gave examples of what distinguished us, such as faith healing and worship styles, but one thing he also said struck me: "Pentecostals don't believe you're saved unless you speak in tongues."

Speak in tongues? I'd noticed that phrase in the Bible a few times now that I was reading it more often, such as in the book of Acts and Paul's letter to the Corinthians. Since it wasn't something I'd seen happen on any level in my church or with other Christians, I just kind of did a mental tune out whenever I read it in my Bible. But this other teenager's question led to a discussion and now a seed was planted in me that night: "Why would those Pentecostal people so arrogantly believe other Christians like me aren't saved? I *know* I'm saved," I thought. "I have Jesus in my life, but I don't speak in tongues or really even know what it is. Those jerks!"

> **"Pentecostals don't believe you're saved unless you speak in tongues."**

Without having even talked to a Pentecostal or so-called Spirit-filled Christian myself yet, I was already offended with them because of the words my youth pastor had spoken. I was now open to believing lies based on hearsay, and, as a result, I'd go on to learn various straw man arguments about the subject of speaking in tongues, many of which we will dismantle in the next section of this book.

At this phase of my life, in my late teens, I had also developed questions on other doctrines from my Bible reading. One of those topics was eternal security and the idea of whether or not a true Christian could lose his or her salvation. I had these questions as I started to highlight passages in my Bible using a certain pen color every time I found warnings about staying strong to the end, or warnings to backsliders to repent. I then proceeded to use another color pen to underline passages in my Bible that dealt with speaking in tongues, as this became the next topic I was curious about and couldn't figure out how to ignore Scripture passages about the subject.

In the months to come, every time I read something about speaking in tongues, I had this nagging doubt in my mind: why is it here in the Bible that the believers in the book of Acts did this if it's not actually a big deal, or if we're not supposed to be doing it anymore? Why is it in the Bible then? It seemed like an honest question for a teenager starting to take the Bible seriously.

I was not nearly as smart at the age of seventeen as I am now as a grown adult (which still isn't necessarily very smart), but I had enough sense to know that if something was in the Bible, I couldn't figure out why people who claimed to believe the Bible would ignore or excuse it. Speaking in tongues seemed to emerge as such a thing that I didn't really understand people's explanations for why not to do it. It ranked right up there with the rapture—another topic people seemed to blindly accept as factual but couldn't really do a good job showing me why they believed a certain way about it, but that's for another book.

> **Why is it here in the Bible that the believers in the book of Acts did this if it's not actually a big deal, or if we're not supposed to be doing it anymore?**

Self-Hypnosis

One more event happened to me as a teenager that tipped me off into not being able to fully buy into those previous explanations anymore. On one Friday night, there was some kind of citywide worship event going on in a rented performing arts center named Market Hall in downtown Peterborough. It was boring and lame as heck. Not just with a capital L, but each letter of lame needs to be capitalized—LAME.

On this one particular night my friend Charles and I decided to walk down to street level and into the Peterborough Square, which was a type of mini-mall in those days beneath Market Hall. I immediately saw a friend of mine from school, whom I knew was a Jewish atheist, arguing and having some kind of shouting match with a man I recognized and knew was a student at the Plymouth Brethren Bible college in my hometown.

From a distance I could tell this was not going well for the Bible college student. I knew my Jewish friend had a good deal of ammunition to use against the gospel since I had tried witnessing to him before. When they stopped and parted ways, I said hi to my friend and then introduced myself to the Bible college student, whom I had just watched lose a shouting match with my friend. We didn't know each other's name, but we recognized each other from events in our denomination that we had both attended. (We knew each other enough that he was relieved to see me—at least I would imagine so after the encounter he had just had.)

I learned that he had been handing out tracts, which are basically small pamphlets that have a simple gospel message presented in them. He and his friends had been hitting the streets looking for people to hand these out to and share the gospel with. That's when he had run into my friend Dave and had gotten into an argument. Throughout the course of talking to him, I decided to ask him his perspective about speaking in tongues. I knew if he was studying the Bible in college he might have an educated answer to the questions I had.

Unfortunately, I was wrong. In his theological answer he insisted that tongues only served a purpose for the early church when the gospel was spreading from outside of Jerusalem and into Samaria. He told me that if you look at the instances when people got baptized in the Holy Spirit in the book of Acts, it followed the pattern given by Jesus where he told his disciples to go with the gospel in Jerusalem, Judea, Samaria, and to the ends of the earth (Acts 1:8). Then after that, those signs that accompanied the spreading of the gospel in Judea, Samaria, and the ends of the earth no longer needed to follow the gospel. I didn't follow his logic at all, but I'm sure he sincerely believed what he told me made sense.

He then began to parrot things he'd clearly been taught but had not learned for himself, since his answer then started to revolve around how another well-known Pentecostal/charismatic church on the edge of town supposedly hypnotized people into thinking they were speaking in tongues. He proceeded to tell me that they have long services and worship for such a long time so that people are more impressionable to be led astray. He furthermore said that when you hear those people speaking in tongues, it's not from the Spirit of God but it's just gibberish and babble. He also used the words "self-hypnosis" several more times in his explanation.

The more he talked the less I believed he had come to this conclusion on his own, but was repeating what one of his professors or pastors had told him. So I asked him if he had ever attended one of these church's services and he admitted he had not, but one of his professors had. Of course one of his professors had! That was the first tip that he might not be worth taking too seriously if the crux of his beliefs on this matter were hearsay from his professors.

> "The power of God? You mean the stuff in the Bible happens today, not just back then in Bible days? That's not what I'd been taught to believe!"

The Brownsville Revival Videos

I didn't give much thought to speaking in tongues again until about a year later, when a friend of mine got back from attending the Brownsville Revival in the summer of 1999. In August, prior to my senior year of high school, Hank (not his real name) came back from having spent the summer in Pensacola, Florida, and a bunch of us all got together at his at-the-time girlfriend's house the next Saturday night for what I was under the impression would be a Bible study. It turned out that Hank had a video of Ken Gott from England preaching at the church he was just attending in Florida. I had never heard preaching like this before. I knew there was a difference in the preaching style of Pentecostals and charismatics I had heard so far, but even that was nothing like what I heard in this video that night.

"The *power* of God? You mean the stuff in the Bible happens today, not just back then in Bible days?" I thought. "That's not what I'd been taught to believe!" Ken Gott shared all these wild testimonies as he preached. We also watched another even more hard-hitting video that night by Michael Rowan, which left many of us in tears in the living room, and in the stadium on the video filled with thousands of youth who were hearing the message live.

I had never heard such powerful preaching before, and after it was over we spent considerable time in prayer. Hank patiently and scripturally explained some things to me about the revival in Pensacola and just what a "revival" was while he drove me home afterward. It sounded awesome and made me wonder how come we didn't have something like that *everywhere* there are Christians (I still wonder this same thing, actually). "What is different about those Christians down there that God is doing this down there and not up here in my hometown, Peterborough?"

And, of course, I had questions for him about speaking in tongues since I saw the speakers in those videos and some people in the living room that night practice it. My theology at the time was of cessationism, which basically believes that the gifts of the Spirit don't happen today, but they were only necessary for the time of the early church. Of course speaking in tongues would be something that cessationists don't expect to happen today.

This night would be the night the dam started to burst open for me.

Note

1. For those readers it would interest, I go into more detail on my blog in a series based on my testimony on a dropdown tab on the homepage.

Chapter 2

Those Crazy Charismatics!

*D*uring my last year of high school, my close buddy Trevor, who was also a leader in our Christian high school group, started "youth group hopping" with me on Friday nights. After a few visits he started accompanying me—or I should say driving me, since I didn't have a car and he had a nice jeep and his driver's license— to the Selwyn Outreach Centre on Friday nights where Hank went. This was also the same church the Bible college student had told me hypnotized people into thinking they were truly speaking in tongues. Anyway, I was convinced if that's where Hank went, I wanted to see what they've got that I was missing, because he was of a different spirit and character than the other Christians I knew. Without knowing exactly what it was, I knew it had everything to do with the whole Pentecostal/charismatic distinction.

I shared my heart with my youth pastor at my home fellowship, and he basically tried talking me out of it, putting an emphasis on the idea that I was jeopardizing my spiritual maturity by going to another youth group instead of "growing where I was planted." I know him well enough to know he was sincere and looking out for my best interests. He may or may not have been right, since as I've matured over the years I can see his point more clearly, but on the other hand I'm glad I didn't listen to him because I never would have experienced things I went on to experience throughout my life. I would have never met some of the people I have met or wound up down the adventurous path on the mission field where I now write this.

> I didn't know how to describe what I was experiencing other than to say that the presence of God was "thicker" here than I had ever sensed before. The speaking and singing in tongues all around me wasn't causing it to feel that way, but I somehow knew the tongue signing was a result of the presence of God.

My first night attending this youth service at Selwyn was marked by amazing worship. I felt so much freer to express myself than I ever did in any other church setting besides Acquire the Fire conference weekends I had attended in the past. There was this one moment where those leading worship and many, if not all, present, began singing in tongues. It was the most beautiful thing I had ever heard, and I thought, "Wow, so that is what it sounds like."

I immediately dismissed what different people had told me about this church, which made me realize most of the Bible college students I'd talked to had probably not even visited this church, or likely *any* charismatic church in their entire lives, for that matter. Otherwise, they wouldn't have been able to slander that congregation to me like the Bible college student had done earlier. It was clearly not a "hypnotic" atmosphere where they "brainwashed me." I didn't know how to describe what I was experiencing other than to say that the presence of God was "thicker" here than I had ever sensed before. The speaking and singing in tongues all around me wasn't causing it to feel that way, but I somehow knew the tongue signing was a result of the presence of God. It was clearly evident these people had something I didn't.

At this point in my life, I started going through my New Living Translation looking for *everything* in the New Testament I could find that dealt with some of the gifts of the Holy Spirit. I underlined passages and circled words with neon colored gel pens for things related to the Holy Spirit and speaking in tongues. I also didn't know anybody else who used these gel pens for any other reason than marking up their Bibles. Hank didn't like my New Living Translation, so he bought me a New King James Version, which I then read through and marked up as well, but using some other color for all the things related to the gifts of the Holy Spirit and charismatic stuff.

In about six months, I had read through the Bible three times. Even though I was only eighteen years old, and still in high school, where much of my studies suffered and my grades were low, I soaked in the Word of God unlike any other season of my life except for Bible college a few years later. I've always had an advanced reading level, so this helped me read the Bible at a pace I considered normal. To my friends, however, I was a reading machine.

> I was interpreting the Bible according to
> my experience instead of changing my
> experience to match the Word of God—
> that's what it all boiled down to.

Hunger for God

I was hungry for more of God, which was unlike anything since the time I got saved and was initially reading the Bible. I started seeing how a lot of what I had been taught was clearly biased and plainly unbiblical. Like everyone else who wants to be honest with themselves, I was interpreting the Bible according to my experience instead of changing my experience to match the Word of God—that's what it all boiled down to. It didn't help that most Christians I was surrounded by didn't even believe in the supernatural aspect of God's character, or they had relegated it to a thing in the past that God "doesn't do anymore."

After this I'd consistently go to the Selwyn church on Friday nights with either Hank or Trevor. I also got addicted to watching borrowed videos of Hank's or another local family who had also attended the Brownsville Revival. By the time I had finished high school, I intended on enrolling in the Brownsville Revival School of Ministry (BRSM). However, some friends who attended or wanted to attend the Pentecostal Bible college in Peterborough gave me cause for concern that on the application prospective students are asked if they speak in tongues or if they've ever been baptized in the Holy Spirit. At that point in time I was open to the charismatic gifts and believed that speaking in tongues was indeed a valid experience Christians could engage in, but I was worried about the possibility of getting denied entry into this school if I didn't speak in tongues. I'd later realize this fear was quite silly.

I didn't wind up going right away, but instead I took a year off after high school to work at a local Subway franchise and save up money for tuition. During this time the BRSM split into two, and an offshoot was formed called FIRE School of Ministry. I applied to both schools, their applications being virtually identical. Since almost the entire faculty went to FIRE after the split, I had made up my mind that I'd rather attend that school since its teachers were in the numerous revival videos I had watched. After all, it was because of them that I decided I wanted to attend and be taught under them for two years of my early adulthood. Neither school's application asked anything about speaking in tongues other than to gauge whether or not the student practiced this in his or her personal life.

You Don't Speak in Tongues?

A high school classmate of mine was also going to attend the FIRE school, so we became close friends for a while. When he found out I didn't speak in tongues, it seemed he went all out to try to convert me to a deeper spiritual life. It was quite suffocating, but I didn't have the heart to tell him I felt this way at the time. I knew he was right, but he overwhelmed me, and many times when we'd get together just to pray or to have fellowship, it seemed speaking in tongues would always come up. I wasn't the one to bring it up, either, if you know what I mean.

> All the charismatics I'd met so far seemed to think I was missing out on something, and part of me knew it was true. However, the aggressive nature of some of my friends to get me to receive the gift of tongues almost smothered me.

From the time that I had started attending Hank's charismatic youth group with my friend Trevor to the time I started classes at FIRE School of Ministry, approximately two years had passed. During this period of time, I had been prayed for by people at least half a dozen times to receive the baptism in the Holy Spirit and nothing seemed to have happened—much to the disappointment and frustration of some of my overzealous Pentecostal friends. I never once spoke in tongues during that two-year period.

My fellow classmate's pushiness was worrying me. I was worried that I might have a difficult time attending a Pentecostal Bible college in Florida for two years without speaking in tongues if everybody was going to be like this with me. I still had all sorts of misconceptions about charismatics and I worried this would be a problem for me if I attended a college in a "revival" atmosphere. All the charismatics I'd met so far seemed to think I was missing out on something, and part of me knew it was true. However, the aggressive nature of some of my friends to get me to receive the gift of tongues almost smothered me. I no longer knew if I even *wanted* to speak in tongues or receive the baptism in the Holy Spirit by this point.

In August of 2001 I carpooled from Peterborough down to Pensacola for a more than twenty-four-hour car ride with two other guys—one in his third year internship with FIRE and the other a classmate I'd enrolled with. I was going the farthest away from home I'd ever gone.

After a couple of days I moved into what would be the house I lived in during my first semester, and right away word spread that "I wasn't filled with the Holy Spirit." It's like everybody was in the same chat room or something about nontongue speakers, because everybody seemed to know that I was the Canadian who didn't speak in tongues. I had one roommate in particular who felt like it was his personal mission to get me filled with the Holy Spirit. His exact words to me were, "How could you attend FIRE and not speak in tongues?" Again, this type of stuff, from the perspective of someone who didn't know, is the very reason why I could have been turned off from ever accepting and receiving this gift.

In the weeks to come, there were a few moments when "the Holy Spirit broke out" in some of our classes and we interceded or people prophesied for the benefit of the whole class. During such moments when people all around me were praying in the Spirit (in other tongues), I didn't get too embarrassed or uncomfortable as I had at previous times. However, I was a little worn out by the zeal of roommates, new classmates, and previous charismatic friends that I remember hoping nobody looked at me during those times and noticed that my lips weren't moving like theirs. I didn't want any more people to take me on as their special project to get filled with the Spirit.

But that all changed after a few weeks.

Chapter 3

September 9, 2001

One night it all came out in front of over six hundred people. Dr. Josh Peters was preaching something out of the second chapter of the book of Acts. Of course he was, because that's all charismatics preach, right? My memory doesn't serve me at this point as to what his message was about or all the points he made, just that at one point he joked that if we really wanted to live out the book of Acts there'd be blood and smoke flowing out of our meetings (Acts 2:17-21). That would sure make people talk about charismatic churches then, wouldn't it?

Toward the end he gave an altar call, asking if there was anybody present who wanted to give their lives to Jesus Christ for the first time. If I remember correctly, there were a couple of people present and they went toward the platform. Then he asked another question: if there was anybody present who wanted to be baptized with the Holy Spirit. I immediately knew the question applied to me, but I looked down and started thinking to myself, "I'm in a new place, with a clean start. Nobody knows very much about me yet. I don't have to let anybody know I'm not 'filled with the Holy Spirit,' which really only meant I didn't need to let anybody know I didn't speak in tongues." Part of me wanted to receive it, "But...not that night. Maybe later after I've had time to process," I thought. "If he asks another night, then on that occasion I'll go forward. Yeah, that's what I'll do.

> Did I **really** want to get prayed for again and **still** not "receive"? Did I really want to go through this ordeal and frustrate a new group of Pentecostals again?

I pondered it for a split second, and my major hindrance was how I'd been prayed for several times in other Pentecostal churches and nothing seemed to have happened and how frustrated the people who prayed over me seemed to get about it. Did I *really* want to get prayed for again and *still* not "receive"? Did I really want to go through this ordeal and frustrate a new group of Pentecostals again? On other occasions people prayed for me for a really long time until they got tired that I wasn't speaking in tongues yet. Did I want to put myself through such frustration again?

Before I could make up my mind, it seemed it was already made up for me. I turned my head and noticed there were arms all around pointed directly at me. I couldn't hide, and Dr. Peters invited me to come down to the area in front of the stage while he encouraged others to come lay hands on me.

Just great. Now everybody in the sanctuary saw me get singled out. Who were all those people pointing at me anyway? I'm sure it was just one or a few people who pointed at me and the rest in that wing of the auditorium also started pointing in the same direction. At any rate, now I was in for it. I was convinced I'd get prayer, that nothing would happen, and then I'd go on my merry way and be an "undercover" charismatic who didn't speak in tongues.

To make matters worse, there had to have been what seemed like about thirty people come down to the altar area to gather around and suffocate me. Okay, they probably didn't want to suffocate me, but when I saw *that* many people ready to gather around and lay hands on me, I was nervous, more than I had ever been before regarding receiving prayer. This is an awful lot of people to let down when I don't wind up speaking in tongues, just like all the other times before.

Did I really want to be here for an hour while people "pressed in" to try to get me to speak in tongues? How do I make up sounds that sound like tongues if it takes too long and I want to go out afterward to eat at Denny's or go straight home? I had all sorts of thoughts run through my head like this, as I was convinced the same thing that had always happened before was going to happen now.

These people began laying hands on me—or at least as many out of that group as could reach me in the multitude—and I felt something flow through my belly that I'd never experienced before or since. It was kind of like a fire, but more like a bubbling up feeling deep in my spirit. I really don't know how to describe it. It was like indigestion, but not painful or uncomfortable. Instead of coming from my esophagus area, it was lower, as though it was in my abdomen. Then there was this type of surge that would go from my abdomen area up to my throat and I'd want to let it out but didn't know how.

Every time I had that sensation—which, by the way, was subtle but still comfortable and not in any way painful or alarming—one of the ladies said, "That's it, that's it, that's it there." I have no idea if I was showing any outward sign of what was going on inside me, but every time I felt that surge pop upward inside me, she would say "that's it" as though she knew exactly what was going on inside of me.

The whole situation lasted only a few moments and many of the people who had gathered around me to pray were now making their way back to their seats. I had a few weird syllables I could now speak out that I couldn't before. It was so simple and felt like it was coming from my stomach instead of from my head. This lady stuck around to encourage me along with a second year student close to my age who encouraged me to keep saying the few syllables that would come up. He told me the more I said them the more the Holy Spirit would provide other words and what sounded like phrases.

Part of me felt ripped off that I didn't experience a more spectacular scene. I really thought some kind of glory ball was supposed to hit me and knock me to the ground and I'd get up speaking in tongues. I can't remember all the misconceptions and false expectations I initially had prior to that night, but this blew me away. That's it? That's all there is to it? I can speak in tongues now? The Holy Spirit doesn't just come down and shake my tongue with his hand and make sounds come out of my mouth? I am in control of whether or not to speak what's coming up from inside me?

When I got home I e-mailed about ten of my friends back in Canada to tell them what had happened. One of them wrote back saying I was *already* baptized in the Spirit, so I was essentially saying I just got saved that night. Another wrote back and encouraged me to use the gift more and I'd see God develop it more in me. So that's what I started to do.

> **Part of me felt ripped off that I didn't experience a more spectacular scene. I really thought some kind of glory ball was supposed to hit me and knock me to the ground and I'd get up speaking in tongues.**

When I prayed the next day during my Monday off, I felt like I was finished praying for everything I could think of in about fifteen minutes or so. If I was going to pray for any prolonged amount of time, then yes, this gift of praying in tongues was going to come in quite handy since I didn't know what else to pray for.

I had this pesky little problem going on in my mind, however—I had only a few syllables that would come out. Even though I was doing this privately in my room, I was still inhibited and thought that maybe this was a joke. Maybe charismatics are just idiots after all and my evangelical friends were right. Maybe I was hypnotizing myself. Oh my goodness, how embarrassing! Tongues can't be this easy! It's supposed to be more spectacular than this!

The next day we had chapel before classes. We would have gone to chapel before classes start like usual, but this was September 11, 2001, and the Twin Trade Towers in New York City had been attacked. I carpooled with two of my roommates that morning to school, and when we arrived there were already a lot of people in the auditorium praying and interceding for what was going on. The details at that hour of the morning were that America was under attack, but it was not known by who or why. I found a corner of the auditorium where I could pray privately since I didn't really know what to do. I almost didn't even believe this had happened, since I didn't own a TV and I am one of the few people I know who didn't watch those towers fall live on TV or the Internet.

> **Tongues can't be this easy! It's supposed to be more spectacular than this!**

I can tell you one thing that I'll never forget about that morning: the prayer language just flowed out of me like a river dam had been destroyed. I no longer only had a few syllables coming out of my mouth. There was no longer just a trickle like the previous twenty-four hours when I tried, but now a mighty flowing river of a new prayer language was coming out of me. Romans 8:26 says that "we do not know what to pray for as we ought, but the Spirit himself intercedes for us with groanings too deep for words." This verse suddenly made sense to me in a much deeper way than ever before since, after all, I quite literally did not know what to pray on the morning of 9/11.

The Walk of the Spirit, the Walk of Power

Later in the fall, months after receiving the baptism in the Holy Spirit and speaking in tongues for the first time, I had another launching pad experience with this gift. I had been regularly speaking in tongues in my worship to God and private prayer times, but I didn't truly understand the value of it until I had my first class with Brian Parkman. He was filling in for two weeks during another class I was taking, and he talked about regularly praying in tongues every day: "Every day, every day, every day," as he'd say.

He told us about a book that would change our lives called *The Walk of the Spirit, The Walk of Power* by Dave Roberson. I had never heard of the author before, and although I knew there was a lot of depth we could plunge into regarding this gift, I couldn't seriously believe anybody could teach enough on it to come up with a four-hundred-page book on the subject. And yet, all these years later, I'm going to cover more stuff in my book that Roberson didn't cover in his.

I was intrigued but it wouldn't be until my second semester when we had a full class with Brian called Principles of Faith and Prayer where we would get a copy of it. When it came weeks later into that semester I read my copy in an entire Saturday. Not just read it, but I took notes in my notepad and highlighted content in the book. It had some good stuff in it, and praying in tongues for prolonged amounts of time became easier and easier to me than it ever had before. This was because I now had a much better understanding of what was going on in my spirit.[1]

Over the years, I've lent my copy of the book to many friends and I have reread it at least once per year. In the last decade it has been worn out and I've noticed it still doesn't necessarily answer everybody's objections as much as it helps stir people up to pray more in the Spirit. I encourage you to read Dave Roberson's book to build yourself up and put into practice what you learn in it and transform your life. And I would also encourage you to keep reading my book if you want to answer your friends who get on your case and tell you different misconceptions about speaking in tongues.

And now, let's tackle the objections.

Note

1. I highly encourage you to get your hands on a copy of that book. This is not some kind of affiliate commission on my part if you buy it, since Dave Roberson's ministry freely gives copies of it away if you call them, or you can get a PDF or Mobi version of it on his website at www.daveroberson.org. Once you read Dave's book, you'll understand the foundation the Lord laid in my life with the practice of speaking in tongues.

Section Two

The Misconceptions

Chapter 4

Pentecostals Believe People Who Don't Speak in Tongues Aren't Saved

I admit I struggled with how I wanted to start off this section of the book, and in which order I wanted to list the misconceptions many people believe. As a result of prayer and carefully thinking it through, as well as receiving the advice of my helpful proofreading friends, I decided I'd start off with this misconception and then in the next chapter we'll get down to some serious Bible exegesis.

The idea that non-Pentecostals aren't saved is something I've heard many times over the years from evangelicals claiming it's what Pentecostals truly do teach. In fact, I've seen some people who believe this get just as indignant as I did the first time I heard that Catholics think Protestants aren't really Christians at all. As my friend and mentor Dr. Stephen Crosby states in his book *Your Empowered Inheritance: Now!*:

Common criticism of Pentecostal and charismatic Christians is their condescending spirit of superiority to those who have not been "Spirit-baptized." This can be, and has been true. Traditional Pentecostal theology is criticized as setting up a two or three tier system of believers—the haves and the have-nots. Much of this criticism is deserved.[1]

I once participated in a discussion on Google+ with a variety of evangelicals about whether or not Pentecostals truly believed this about other denominations. One man in this discussion was evidently a Baptist pastor whom an Assemblies of God church had once invited to come preach. However, when this pastor visited their website, he found they believed in the baptism in the Holy Spirit subsequent to salvation, including the sign or evidence of speaking in tongues. He decided upon learning this to decline their invitation because he deduced this meant they believed people aren't saved unless they speak in tongues.

I tried dialoguing and showing him that *he* was the one concluding they believed that, but they probably didn't or else they wouldn't have invited him to preach to their fellowship. He didn't know how ironic his reason for rejecting a preaching invitation was on his part, and that it was possible he was shutting a door that God might have been opening for him to share with that flock of which they wouldn't have received through anybody else but him.

I hear quite often how allegedly we charismatics are divisive. Historically, this accusation is deserved. However, I personally encounter divisiveness more often than not with people who would not subscribe to my understanding of the charismatic gifts. I've had evangelicals and Baptists place walls up between themselves and me in certain ministry and mission settings that had never crossed my mind to be divisive over or make a big deal out of.

I've been in corporate prayer meetings while we petition God for something and I resisted praying in my prayer language in front of them. Later someone came up to me and told me, "I'm so glad you didn't erupt into tongues, because that would have been inappropriate unless someone interpreted. We're so glad you kept that to yourself, Steve." I then take a moment to show even more restraint by not asking them why they even bothered to mention this to me in the first place. Maybe some have been so burned in the past by the foolishness and immaturity of some overzealous charismatics that they're ready to react and pounce on the next one they come across? I truly don't know.

> **"Those Pentecostals believe you need to speak in tongues in order to be saved." Usually the Pentecostals would tell me, "Of course you're still saved even if you don't speak in tongues!"**

On another occasion prior to that Internet discussion, I had just finished watching a YouTube video of a guy teaching about speaking in tongues who went around in circles with his reasoning when preaching to his church. I couldn't tell who exactly he was addressing, but he admonished them that if any of them are ever around a charismatic who teaches that you need to speak in tongues in order to truly be saved, to get the heck away from them.

This made me think of different misconceptions I used to have about charismatics, like I mentioned in earlier in this book, such as this particular lie about our view of their salvation. I grew up attending a Plymouth Brethren church. This particular fellowship is a lot more open and progressive now than in years passed, and in comparison to other churches in their denomination. I maintain some close friendships to this day as a result of not burning any kind of bridges with them or letting theological differences get in the way of true friendships. However, that doesn't stop some of the things dear saints have told me over the years from being untrue.

My hometown of Peterborough used to have two different Bible colleges. One was a Brethren college and the other was Canada's largest denominational Bible college for a number of years, which of course was Pentecostal. I volunteered for a couple of years at a youth drop-in called The Bridge Youth Centre (that is spelled correctly, because in Canada we spell Center with the R and *then* the E, just in case you were about to throw this book away for having such an embarrassing typo). At any rate, I used to work with a lot of students from both Bible colleges who were doing ministry or internships for credit in their schools. As a result, I got confused sometimes when I asked different students questions on various Bible doctrines that I came to find out they disagreed on. Many people from the Brethren Bible college taught me "those Pentecostals believe you need to speak in tongues in order to be saved." So what did I do? I asked the Pentecostal students myself when I saw them during my shifts at the drop-in. I was only eighteen years old, but I've always had a desire to get to the bottom of things. Usually the Pentecostals would tell me, "Of course you're still saved even if you don't speak in tongues!"

At the time of writing this I've been a Christian for over sixteen years and still have never actually come across *any* charismatic, or someone who'd call themselves one, state they believe that I or anybody else was not saved while we was unable to speak in tongues. But that's not to say that there are no groups and denominations out there that do in fact feel this way, but they are not representative of all Pentecostals or charismatics.

The confusion about this matter comes into play often when believers combine the baptism in the Holy Spirit with the salvation experience itself. So if I were to say tongues accompanies the baptism in the Spirit, and a hearer believes that the baptism of the Spirit has already happened at salvation, it sounds like I am stating the other believer is not truly a Christian. Otherwise, by and large the misconception we're basing this chapter on is not nearly as widespread as I've been able to find from research.

> **It was not the desire to disobey God that separated us from him, but our desire to try and be righteous on our own that separated us from him.**

Salvation Is Not Dependent on Speaking in Tongues

I'm assuming you are probably already a Christian if you're reading this book, and that you may already know how you came to know the Lord Jesus Christ. However, I want to take a moment before moving forward, as a Pentecostal myself, to explain what I believe the gospel is and how someone gets saved, just in case for some reason you picked up this book thinking it was something else and you read this far and don't have a clue what I'm talking about.

When man sinned in the garden of Eden, he was not punished for smoking a joint or having sex outside of marriage. Adam didn't get drunk with his friends while chasing women around. What he and Eve tried to do was *good* outside of the parameters of what the Lord instructed.

It was not the desire to disobey God that separated us from him, but our desire to try and be righteous on our own that separated us from him. Eve was led astray out of the desire to *be like* God, and they ate of the fruit, believing the serpent's lie that she'd be just like God if she ate. Humanity banished themselves from God's presence trying to do things *their own way* instead of God's prescribed way. It was their desire to do what was *perceived* as good but was in fact disobedience that got them kicked out of the garden.

What happened when they ate the fruit God told them not to eat? "Then the eyes of both were opened, and they knew that they were naked. And they sewed fig leaves together and made themselves loincloths" (Genesis 3:7). What does God think of our efforts to be good on our own, and cover our sins with clothing of our own making? Isaiah 64:6 mentions how our own self-righteous deeds are like filthy rags, and Paul says in Romans 3:10 that none are righteous.

Jesus said, "Whoever looks at a woman to lust after her, has committed adultery with her in his heart" (Matthew 5:28). Have you ever lied or stolen, even small things, or looked at someone with lust? Most people are guilty of *just* those three, and there are still seven other commandments to take into consideration when considering the law of God. Failure at just one of these points makes us guilty of breaking all of God's law. You will be guilty on the day of judgment and therefore end up in hell. That's not God's desired will, however (2 Peter 3:9).

In response to this, God the Father sent his Son Jesus Christ to take your punishment: "God commanded His love toward us, in that, while we were yet sinners, Christ died for us" (Romans 5:8, NKJV). To receive God's gift of everlasting life, one needs only to ask him. I encourage you to pray something like this if what I'm talking about applies to you:

> *Dear God, I repent of all my sins (it might be a good idea to name them here). This day I put my trust in Jesus Christ as my Lord (Master) and Savior. Please forgive me and grant me your gift of everlasting life, which is your Son Jesus. In his name, I pray. Amen.*

Then read the Bible daily and obey what you read. Pray in tongues often as well. If you don't know how to do that yet, then keep reading this book.

Maybe you are reading this and don't know Jesus for yourself and you picked up this book thinking you'd discover something else in it. You may be struggling with understanding that if God truly is so loving, then how could he ever send a single soul to hell? Maybe the "god" in your imagination and your perception of who he is wouldn't. That is idolatry, making a god in your own image. However, the God of the Bible is so holy, the question is not how could a loving God send anyone to hell, but how could such a holy God *let* any impure and sinful people into heaven? The answer is only by his grace and unmerited favor, through the blood his Son Jesus Christ shed on the cross to pay the penalty we deserve.

Romans 6:23 says that "the wages of sin is death, but the free gift of God is eternal life in Christ Jesus our Lord." If you've ever held a job, you received wages in the form of a paycheck or deposit into your bank account when payday came. A wage literally is what you are owed in exchange for what you've done (the work for your employer). Simply put, because of what you and I have done, God *owes* us death as a punishment. But because of his overwhelming love for us, Jesus Christ paid that price for us on the cross. The choice is yours as to whether or not you will decide to submit to him and stop trying to be good on your own.

> **Saying you're not saved unless you do something, in this case speak in tongues, subtly says that because you're doing something then you're saved.**

That being said, to tie this back into speaking in tongues, let's remember that we were not able to earn our salvation. I have yet to personally meet a Pentecostal or charismatic whose doctrine on salvation hinges on speaking in tongues. If it did, then it would fly in the face of God's unmerited favor toward us and our inability to earn our own salvation. Saying you're not saved unless you do something, in this case speak in tongues, subtly says that because you're doing something then you're saved. This is obvious but bears stating plainly, since otherwise it would imply that God's salvation is conditional. We know it's not based on any condition other than accepting it and letting him wash us clean unto repentance.

Maybe you've stated this and didn't mean it quite how I just worded it, to imply that tongues causes salvation, but you merely think tongues is the fruit or evidence that salvation has taken place in an individual's heart. That is equally untrue. You do need the Holy Spirit in order to truly speak in tongues, but you don't need to speak in tongues in order to have the Holy Spirit.[2] In the next chapter we will explore the baptism in the Holy Spirit and how it's a separate work that occurs any time after salvation.

Notes

1. Stephen R. Crosby, *Your Empowered Inheritance: Now!* (Stephanos Ministries), 172.

2. We will explore this further as we go along. In a later chapter we will also explore more in-depth that since we can speak in tongues at will, it's even more obvious that it can't be something we do to earn or obtain our own salvation, or even favor from God.

Chapter 5

Holy Spirit Baptism Already Happened at Salvation

When I first got baptized in the Holy Spirit and spoke in tongues for the first time in Bible college, I remember getting mixed reactions when I wrote to several friends back home in Canada. Of those who didn't believe in speaking in tongues, the response in the e-mails would be things like "Congrats on finally getting saved, Steve!"

This was obviously a sarcastic jab, since the people I wrote to all knew that I was a believer. I was at B-i-b-l-e college—they don't just let anybody go to those, you know! For some of my friends, this was a subtle but sarcastic way of making sure I knew they believed the baptism in the Holy Spirit already happened at salvation and it was not some subsequent experience one had after already being saved.

I wanted to make the focus of this book on *only* speaking in tongues and not all of the gifts of the Spirit, or even specifically Spirit baptism. However, I realized it would be a disservice to speak in-depth about tongues without covering what usually is the starting point for most believers who practice this in their prayer lives. This book really wouldn't flow if I neglected to tackle this as a post-conversion experience for all believers who want it.

I want to make clear at the outset that there are entire books that cover this subject in a broader way when it comes to the Holy Spirit and his work in salvation and baptism. This chapter will cover my points in more of a summary of the subject or a cursory overview.

> There is only one baptism **in Christ** that all Christians are baptized into. There is only one **salvation** in Christ Jesus. However, I seem to be able to find three different baptisms in the New Testament.

Three Baptisms in the Bible

That being said, one of the first things people often tell me when correcting my understanding of this subject, that this is called the *baptism* in the Holy Spirit, is to point out that all believers are already baptized into Christ. When saying this, they are referring to what Paul wrote to the Ephesians:

> *There is one body and one Spirit—just as you were called to the one hope that belongs to your call— one*

> *Lord, one faith,* **one baptism,** *one God and Father of all, who is over all and through all and in all.* (Ephesians 4:4-7)

"Aha! See, Steve, it says right there that there's only one baptism!" they suggest. And to that I say yes, there is only one baptism *in Christ* that all Christians are baptized into. There is only one *salvation* in Christ Jesus. There is only one burial and resurrection through the blood of God's Son. We are in agreement about that. However, I seem to be able to find three different baptisms in the New Testament.

The first is the already-mentioned baptism "into" Christ, which is also mentioned in 1 Corinthians 12:12-13:

> *For just as the body is one and has many members, and all the members of the body, though many, are one body, so it is with Christ.* **For in one Spirit we were all baptized into one body**—*Jews or Greeks, slaves or free—and all were made to drink of one Spirit.*

Through the Holy Spirit we are all baptized into Christ's body, who is the head, and who is our Savior. By confessing that Jesus is Lord and believing with our hearts that he has made us new—and has "baptized us" in him—we all have *this* baptism in our salvation experience. There is only one of *these* baptisms. However, we also see a baptism "in" water (Acts 8:38), which is our verification with Christ in his burial (Colossians 2:12; Romans 6:3-4). We are not baptized in water the exact moment when we're saved, but when we allow ourselves to be baptized in water, we are symbolically showing in a public way that we have died to our old selves and have been resurrected in Christ.

The third baptism in Scripture is the baptism of the Holy Spirit (Acts 2:4). It is not related to salvation but it is for the power to be a witness for the Lord Jesus Christ (Luke 24:49). Jesus Christ himself is the baptizer in the Spirit (John 1:32-33; Matthew 3:11). In a manner of speaking, the same way an individual such as your pastor or leader or maybe the person who led you to Christ might be there to lower you into physical water when you are born again, Jesus does the same to us by his Spirit. Only instead of using water, he uses the Holy Spirit. This imagery may not sit well with some, and it is not perfect, but it's how I picture it for our illustration here. This baptism is not connected to initiation into Christ like the first baptism, but is an empowering for Christian service.

The Holy Spirit likewise didn't give half of a baptism at our salvation, and then if we're lucky and decide we want to be Pentecostal, we can receive prayer and get the second half of the baptism. Nor is the Holy Ghost a set of twins, and we get one of them at salvation and the other during a post-conversion experience. There is *one* Holy Spirit. The believer is complete upon salvation and not deficient in any way whatsoever.

However, the function and outworking of these two processes are quite different. One experience is an indwelling *in* us for our personal life, producing spiritual fruit. The other is the Holy Spirit coming *upon* us for power and service toward others, resulting in enablements or spiritual gifts. We also need to realize that the Holy Spirit is a person and not a set of experiences or neat theological categories.

The Purpose of the Baptism in the Holy Spirit

I'm not sure who this quote comes from, but it's been said that "the baptism of the Holy Spirit is not something to have, but something to use. It is not the height of spiritual experience, but one of the tremendously essential foundations for further development and service."[1] Everything a Christian needs to live a godly life in Christ has been provided for us in Christ the instant we are born again.[2] Spirit baptism is a supernatural equipping with power from heaven to empower the Christian for effective witness and service.

> **The Holy Spirit is a person and not a set of experiences or neat theological categories.**

In his book *The Charismatic Theology of St Luke: Trajectories from the Old Testament to Luke-Acts*, Roger Stronstad states about this baptism:

> In regard to their future prophethood Jesus promised his disciples (1) that God would give his Spirit to those who asked him (Luke 11:13), (2) that the Spirit would inspire words of defense when the disciples suffered persecution (12:12; 21:14, 15), (3) that the Spirit would empower their witness (24:49; Acts 1:8), and (4) that they would be baptized in the Holy Spirit (as the Father had earlier promised through John the Baptist, Acts 1:4-5). These promises begin to be filled on the post-Easter day of Pentecost when Jesus pours out his Spirit of prophecy upon the company of about 120 disciples (Acts 2:1-21). What happens on the day of Pentecost is a transfer of the Spirit from Jesus himself to his disciples (Acts 2:33). By this transfer

of the Spirit Jesus's disciples become a community of Spirit-baptized, Spirit-empowered, and Spirit-filled prophets (Acts 1:5, 8; 2:4, 17-21).[3]

And furthermore, Stronstad writes, "Therefore, just as the mission of Jesus was inaugurated in the power of the Spirit, so at Pentecost the mission of the disciples will be inaugurated in the power of the Spirit."[4]

One of my favorite concepts I've ever heard to describe the "dual" working of the Holy Spirit both in and on the believer is like inhaling and exhaling air. Dr. Frank D. Macchia, speaking of Luke the gospel writer and author of the Acts of the Apostles, puts it like this:

> The breath of God through Pentecost inhales the people into God's holy presence and exhales them outward into deliverance for the sick and the oppressed. The penultimate fulfillment of Spirit baptism for Luke is akin to a prophetic call that draws people close to the heart of God in praise and prophetic empathy in order to empower them for witness in the world.
>
> For Luke, Spirit baptism does *not only* purge and indwell so that the people of God can be a holy temple, it empowers so that they may also function as a living witness. The flame of the Spirit that burns within God's people as a holy temple is a spreading flame.[5]

Macchia also previously mentions in his book that the Spirit baptism in Luke does not just cleanse the temple (the believer) as John's baptism symbolized, but it fills the temple with God's holy presence.

Time-Lapse between Salvation and Spirit Baptism

Let's quickly skim through the book of Acts and look at how each "baptism," "outpouring," or "filling," or whatever exact term you want to use, took place subsequent to conversion.

> *Jesus said to them again, "Peace be with you. As the Father has sent me, even so I am sending you." And when he had said this, he breathed on them and said to them, "Receive the Holy Spirit."* (John 20:21-22)

Scholars as well as individuals with an educated opinion are split on just what is meant here toward the end of John's Gospel account where Jesus made this statement. Some say he was sending them the indwelling of the Holy Spirit, breathing into them the same way God breathed life into the dust of the earth when he formed Adam. I'm personally not going to be dogmatic about it, but as we segue into the book of Acts, written by detail-oriented Luke the physician, we see in the first few verses before Jesus ascended up into heaven that he told the disciples to stay and not leave Jerusalem. Why were they to do this?

> *And while staying with them he ordered them not to depart from Jerusalem, but to wait for the promise of the Father, which, he said, "you heard from me; for John baptized with water, but you will be baptized with the Holy Spirit not many days from now."* (Acts 1:4-5)

These same individuals whom Jesus breathed on and told to receive the Holy Spirit were now told to wait in Jerusalem until they were baptized with the Holy Spirit. Whether the breathing on them mentioned at the end of John's Gospel refers to the indwelling or not, it's interesting to note they were going to receive a second experience, both of which involved the Holy Spirit. Just before ascending up into the clouds, Jesus explained the purpose of this second experience they would receive:

> *But you will receive power when the Holy Spirit has come upon you, and you will be my witnesses in Jerusalem and in all Judea and Samaria, and to the end of the earth.* (Acts 1:8)

At the end Luke's Gospel, Jesus told the disciples to wait and not leave Jerusalem until they received this promise from the Father (Luke 24:49). Keep in mind that Jesus had just told them to wait for the promised Holy Spirit to come after they'd already been saved. He had encouraged them earlier in his earthly ministry to ask the Father for the Holy Spirit: "If you then, who are evil, know how to give good gifts to your children, how much more will the heavenly Father give the Holy Spirit to those who ask him" (Luke 11:13).

We know that a person cannot be saved if not for the work of God's Spirit, and all Christians are temples of the Holy Spirit:

> *Therefore I want you to understand that no one speaking in the Spirit of God ever says "Jesus is accursed!" and no one can say "Jesus is Lord" except in the Holy Spirit.* (1 Corinthians 12:3)

> *Or do you not know that your body is a temple of the Holy Spirit within you, whom you have from God? You are not your own.* (1 Corinthians 6:19)

You, however, are not in the flesh but in the Spirit, if in fact the Spirit of God dwells in you. Anyone who does not have the Spirit of Christ does not belong to him. (Romans 8:9)

> **Jesus told the disciples to tarry in Jerusalem until they received power, and he did not tell them to wait until they "got saved," "reborn," "regenerated," or any other synonym we may use to describe the Holy Spirit's work in our lives upon salvation.**

It's clear that the purpose of what they were to wait for had to do with being an effective witness for Jesus after he ascended to heaven. Of this Stronstad states:

> In addition, as one interpreter has observed, "Luke records at least fifteen conversion accounts in Acts, and not one of these is described as a baptism in the Spirit." Therefore, when judged against either Luke's "antecedent spiritual state" narrative strategy, or by Luke's fifteen conversion accounts, interpreters who assert that Luke's "baptized in the Holy Spirit" narratives are about conversion-initiation are guilty of twisting Luke's data for their own theological ends.[6]

The baptism in the Holy Spirit is not synonymous for receiving the Holy Spirit upon salvation. Jesus told the disciples to tarry in Jerusalem until they received power, and he did not tell them to wait until they "got saved," "reborn," "regenerated," or any other synonym we may use to describe the Holy Spirit's work in our lives upon salvation. They were showing evidence of salvation already when they met to pray in the upper room every day until that God-ordained day of Pentecost. And just in case you think otherwise, let me remind you how rare it is to find unbelievers gathering in groups to pray every day to God.

The explanations I've been given or heard to explain otherwise take interpretive and logical acrobatics in order to hold water, and, for brevity's sake, they aren't persuasive enough for me to list and refute in this chapter. But that's beside the point. You'd be right in pointing out to me that all throughout history there have been great men of God who were ministers of the church before getting saved, such as John and Charles Wesley. People can serve and be going through the motions of spiritual activities without personally knowing Christ as Savior. However, of those gathered, at least in the case of the eleven disciples Jesus had breathed on earlier, they had already received something from the Holy Spirit, and now, on the day of Pentecost, they received something else altogether.

The Day of Pentecost

When the day of Pentecost arrived, they were all together in one place. And suddenly there came from heaven a sound like a mighty rushing wind, and it filled the entire house where they were sitting. And divided tongues as of fire appeared to them and rested on each one of them. And they were all filled with the Holy Spirit and began to speak in other tongues as the Spirit gave them utterance. (Acts 2:1-4)

Notice that in the previous chapter mention is made of one hundred and twenty believers being present when Judas was replaced as one of the twelve apostles (Acts 1:14-16). For this reason many have assumed that all of these individuals were present in the upper room approximately ten days later. Since Scripture is not definitive regarding this detail, I'm not going to be dogmatic one way or the other. Some have speculated and went so far as to say that only the twelve disciples received the tongues of fire on their heads and spoke in tongues. To me, it's neither here nor there whether there were twelve or one hundred and twenty. The fact remains that some are clearly receiving a definite second experience here.[7]

Toward the beginning of Acts 8, we see the account of Philip sharing the gospel and starting a revival of sorts in Samaria. Notice that Philip was not one of the twelve apostles, but one of the deacons appointed to serve tables and to free the apostles up to do more preaching (Acts 6:5). Why is it significant that Philip was preaching in Samaria? Well, do you remember how surprised the woman at the well was when Jesus was talking to her, because Jews didn't associate with Samaritans (John 4:9)? Here we are, years later, and at least this Jew, Philip, was now preaching the gospel to them. His message was supported with signs and wonders beyond anything that they had seen before. Unclean spirits were cast out, and paralyzed and lame people were healed (Acts 8:6-8). But they were not all filled or baptized with the Holy Spirit just yet.

> *Now when the apostles at Jerusalem heard that Samaria had received the word of God, they sent to them Peter and John, who came down and prayed for them that they might receive the Holy Spirit, for he had not yet fallen on any of them, but they had only been baptized in the name of the Lord Jesus. Then*

they laid their hands on them and they received the Holy Spirit. (Acts 8:14-17)

> We're talking several days, if not weeks, between when the Samaritans accepted the message Philip preached, and when they received the baptism in Holy Spirit. This was clearly a second, post-conversion experience.

We need to remember that this was the first century AD. When we read the Bible text, especially glancing over a few sentences, we can forget to realize how much time something may have taken in the narrative. We must keep in mind that in those days, they didn't have radio, TV, or Internet. Philip didn't whip out his iPhone and upload a photo to Facebook. He didn't film the Samaritan revival and upload a video to YouTube for his church buddies in Jerusalem to see. This took time. In those days, communication happened as fast as a messenger could ride a horse.

A straight-line distance from Jerusalem to Samaria (or the other way around, of course) is about thirty-five miles. If you look at any map in the back of your Bible, you'll see it might indicate close to forty. There's little likelihood the path one would take in those days would be perfectly straight. So if we think of the time it took for word to get back to Jerusalem, which is about however long it takes to travel that distance on foot, horse, or camel, we are then left with the fact these individuals in Samaria were saved for a while before the other apostles traveled to their town to further minister to them.

Plus, add to that the amount of time the church in Jerusalem might have spent praying and discussing the Samaria situation and picking which disciples would get to go on that mission to follow up on it. Let's also not forget that now Peter and John traveled there and spent time with these new converts and prayed for them to receive the Holy Spirit. Add all of that up, and we're talking several days, if not weeks, between when the Samaritans accepted the message Philip preached, and when they received the baptism in Holy Spirit when Peter and John laid hands on them. This was clearly a second, post-conversion experience for the Samaritans.

Concerning the Samaritan reception of the Holy Spirit, Stronstad states:

> The Samaritan narrative confronts the reader with the chronological separation between the belief of the Samaritans and their reception of the Spirit. Not only did their faith fail to effect the reception of the Spirit, but their baptism likewise failed to be the locus of their reception of the Spirit. This is a vexing theological problem for many interpreters, for it contradicts their theological presuppositions concerning the baptism in the Holy Spirit.[8]

Chronologically, the next incident of Spirit baptism in the book of Acts is when the apostle Paul was converted on the road to Damascus when he had a personal visitation of the Lord and then received prayer by Ananias three days later. Luke writes:

> *So Ananias departed and entered the house. And laying his hands on him he said, "Brother Saul, the Lord Jesus who appeared to you on the road by*

which you came has sent me so that you may regain your sight and be filled with the Holy Spirit." (Acts 9:17)

If one were to look at the apostle Paul's conversion, it appears that he was filled with the Holy Spirit upon conversion. Whether or not we can say he received Christ and committed to following him the first time the Lord spoke to him three days prior, or whether it was here when Ananias laid hands on him and prayed, is subject to interpretation. At any rate, scales fell from his eyes when Ananias prayed for him. Whether literal or figurative scales we don't know, but now Paul could see again and would never be the same.

In the next chapter, Peter preaches the gospel to those in Cornelius's household and we see salvation, water baptism, and speaking in tongues in the same instances of conversion. In my opinion, that is ideal. In Acts 10:34-43 we're given a concise summary of what Peter preached to the Gentiles. Then things changed during Peter's sermon:

*While Peter was still saying these things, the Holy Spirit fell on all who heard the word. And the believers from among the circumcised who had come with Peter were amazed, because the gift of the Holy Spirit was poured out even on the Gentiles. For they were hearing them speaking in tongues and extolling God. Then Peter declared, "Can anyone withhold water for baptizing these people, **who have received the Holy Spirit just as we have?"** And he commanded them to be baptized in the name of Jesus Christ. Then they asked him to remain for some days.* (Acts 10:44-48)

Take note of the order that things happened here. First, Peter preached and the Holy Spirit "fell on all who heard the word." Second, the Gentiles who received the Holy Spirit spoke in tongues and extolled God. Then Peter declared that they should be baptized in water in the name of Jesus Christ. Then last of all, Peter seems to have stayed a few days longer. We can only speculate what he did or what more he taught in that period of time.

> **It is not always necessary for there to be a delay or a pause in the time from which someone accepts Jesus Christ as their Lord and Savior until the point when they speak in tongues for the first time.**

Notice in Peter's question to the other Jewish believers present with him about who could stop the Gentiles from being baptized since they had just received the Holy Spirit like they themselves previously had. How exactly did Peter and the other disciples receive? If we go back to Acts 2, they experienced a mighty rushing wind, tongues of fire over their heads, and they all spoke in other tongues as the Spirit prompted them. It wouldn't be a stretch to assume that the Holy Spirit being poured out on the Gentiles on this occasion may have been just as spectacular of an event. But one thing is certain: there was obviously a similarity that Peter and the Jews present could pinpoint that had also happened when they received the Holy Spirit on the day of Pentecost. It's my contention that at the very least, it would be the tongues speaking.

It is not always necessary for there to be a delay or a pause in the time from which someone accepts Jesus Christ as their Lord and Savior until the point when they speak in tongues for the first time. The Gentiles were fortunate enough to have the experiences coincide at the same time. However, several chapters later, we see believers receive the Holy Spirit, speak in tongues, and prophesy after a much longer interval—as long as twenty years!

> And it happened that while Apollos was at Corinth, Paul passed through the inland country and came to Ephesus. There he found some disciples. And he said to them, "**Did you receive the Holy Spirit when you believed**?" And they said, "No, we have not even heard that there is a Holy Spirit." And he said, "Into what then were you baptized?" They said, "Into John's baptism." And Paul said, "John baptized with the baptism of repentance, telling the people to believe in the one who was to come after him, that is, Jesus." On hearing this, they were baptized in the name of the Lord Jesus. And **when Paul had laid his hands on them, the Holy Spirit came on them**, and they began speaking in tongues and prophesying. (Acts 19:1-6)

Paul ran into individuals who had been disciples of John the Baptizer for longer than he had been saved. Upon encountering them, he asked them if they received the Holy Spirit when they believed. Now why would Paul have asked this question if, by default, everybody receives this when they believe in Christ? Obviously Paul's understanding of the Holy Spirit is shown here, and he proceeds to lay hands on them and bring them into a further experience that he felt they were missing out on. Not to mention that when he did so, they spoke in tongues and prophesied, both of which are external vocal evidences that something had happened.

Summary

In conclusion, even if we just give a cursory glance to these experiences documented in the book of Acts, we can easily conclude that the experience of the Holy Spirit that Jesus was telling his disciples to ask for in Acts 1 is something different from what every Christian experiences upon his or her salvation. If we're automatically going to receive it when we're saved, or regenerated, what is the point in telling us to ask for it or seek after it?

The Spirit already indwells all believers when they make a commitment to accept Christ and make him Lord of their life. Spirit baptism is an additional work of the already indwelling Holy Spirit. The empowerment that comes with the baptism in the Spirit is to strengthen their witness with other gifts and signs and wonders. As a result, the manifestation of tongues usually tends to accompany it.

Notes

1. Source unknown.

2. For more about the "seed" that has been planted in us, my e-book *The Imperishable Seed of Christ* covers this way more in-depth than I wish to here.

3. Roger Stronstad, The Charismatic Theology of St Luke: Trajectories from the Old Testament to Luke-Acts (Baker Academic), Location 1146, Kindle.

4. Ibid., Location 1253.

5. Frank D. Macchia, Baptized in the Spirit: A Global Pentecostal Theology (Zondervan), 101.

6. Stronstad, The Charismatic Theology of St Luke, Location 1366, Kindle.

7. We will look more in a later chapter about how difficult it would be for any of the onlookers below to pinpoint their own language being spoken in the midst of the commotion.

8. Stronstad, The Charismatic Theology of St Luke, Location 1493.

Chapter 6

Tongues Are Not for Today

*M*any believers might accept the points presented in the previous chapter about the baptism in the Holy Spirit being a second experience after salvation; however, many stop there and have various reasons for why they believe it was only for the early church. I have even heard people get frustrated with me for "failing to see" that this was meant only to inaugurate the church on the earth, and that after that time there was no reason to expect the continuation of signs, wonders, miracles, or the gifts of the Holy Spirit. There are many in the body of Christ who disagree that the use of tongues is for the church throughout all the ages, insisting that it was only intended for the early church as part of the foundational signs and wonders that would accompany the gospel's spread to the Gentile world.

At this point it would be worth a moment to give some definitions. First, glossolalia comes from the Greek *glōssa*, meaning "tongue," and *lalia*, meaning "talking," and that also sometimes refers to xenoglossy, which involves the speaking of a natural language previously unknown to the speaker. The term cessationist is used to describe someone who believes that the miraculous gifts of the Holy Spirit ceased with the death of the last apostle or shortly thereafter. Glossolalia, in particular, is also excluded from everyday charismatic use since its purpose would have ceased also after this period.

This common viewpoint in evangelicalism holds that the gifts of the Holy Spirit as laid out in the apostle Paul's first letter to the Corinthians were to inaugurate and initiate, but not to be normative for the life of the church thereafter. That is to say they served a purpose only for the early church when it was being birthed, and then they were never needed again after that. However, this makes about as much sense as saying milk and solid food are only for babies in their infancy and then after that they don't eat ever again.

A key text its proponents use is 1 Corinthians 13:8-12:

> *Love never ends. As for prophecies, they will pass away; as for tongues, they will cease; as for knowledge, it will pass away. For we know in part and we prophesy in part, but when the perfect comes, the partial will pass away. When I was a child, I spoke like a child, I thought like a child, I reasoned like a child. When I became a man, I gave up childish ways. For now we see in a mirror dimly, but then face to face. Now I know in part; then I shall know fully, even as I have been fully known.*

I don't wish to make generalizations about my brothers and sisters in Christ, so it would do me well to acknowledge that not all of my friends and colleagues who dismiss contemporary use of the gifts of the Holy Spirit would consider themselves to be cessationists. Many would consider themselves open to the Holy Spirit but cautious of the use of the gifts, believing that they did not cease after the first century, but that much of what is purported to be operations of the spiritual gifts today are suspect.

Suffice it to say, a large enough number of believers who don't consider themselves to be Pentecostal or charismatic subscribe to the view I'm about to explain, and believe that the "perfect" being spoken of in verse 10 is the completion of the Bible. Therefore, under this outlook, yes, speaking in tongues and prophesying would happen but only until the perfect has arrived, which is referred to and believed by them to be the completion of the canon of Scripture.

> **The charismatic view is that all of the gifts and ministries of the Spirit are still in operation today, building up the body until the fullness of Christ is reached since we are clearly not seeing Jesus face to face yet.**

They say that now that the Bible has been completed we do not need the gifts of the Spirit, so the gifts have passed away as their purpose is no longer needed. To cessationists, the early church was immature and childish (Ephesians 4:11-13), and the gifts and ministries of the Holy Spirit were given to help mature the church in its infancy. Now that the church is fully grown, and, in particular, now that it has the Bible, the things which initially caused this growth are no longer needed the same way an adult no longer needs to be breastfed or have his or her diapers changed. The gifts merely served a purpose for a season.

Charismatics and Pentecostals, on the other hand, interpret this passage with the understanding that the "perfect" speaks of the fulfillment of the ages, when we as believers will see Jesus face to face. The gifts were given to grow and mature the church into the body and image of Jesus Christ. The Bible is the written Word that guides us in the ministries and functions of the gifts, and serves as an important aid in the Christian's life. The charismatic view is that all of the gifts and ministries of the Spirit are still in operation today, building up the body until the fullness of Christ is reached since we are clearly not seeing Jesus face to face yet.

In my dialoguing and interacting with various friends who hold to a cessationist view, as well as doing much reading on the subject over the years, I've come to find that my evangelical friends will acknowledge and confirm that, yes, each time in the book of Acts whenever believers received the baptism in the Holy Spirit, they spoke in tongues. However, the cessationist declares that it stops there and was only meant to happen in the inauguration stages of the church. After that, the different sign gifts were no longer needed because we now have the Bible. Understanding the context of Paul's letter to the Corinthians is important for understanding correctly what he was saying to them.

The previous chapters detail various concerns Paul had for the Corinthians, such as lawsuits, sexual immorality, and the improper use of liberty, which prevented them from functioning as a local fellowship in a trustworthy and mature way. This brings us to the twelfth chapter of his letter on the proper use of spiritual gifts.

Before we tackle this particular issue, we need to realize Paul is writing a corrective letter to a specific local fellowship. He's already stated that what he was telling them was in fact milk (1 Corinthians 3:2), and not solid food, because they were not ready to handle what "meat" he had intended on sharing with them. That's to say, he's getting down to the basics with them and not going further than that. Compare Paul's remark in First Corinthians 3 to what he says to the Jewish believers in the book of Hebrews:

> *About this we have much to say, and it is hard to explain, since you have become dull of hearing. For though by this time you ought to be teachers, you need someone to teach you again the basic principles of the oracles of God. You need milk, not solid food, for* **everyone who lives on milk is unskilled in the word of righteousness,** *since he is a child. But solid food is for the mature, for those who have their powers of discernment trained by constant practice to distinguish good from evil.* (Hebrews: 5:11-14)

If the Corinthians were also unskilled in the word of righteousness and living on milk, then we also are forced to come to a realization that operating in the gifts of the Spirit are not signs of maturity, since these individuals were using the gifts but needed to be corrected in their use.

As a Bible teacher living in Peru, I understand the idea of finding clear ways to communicate or teach something that I feel is profound. Many times I'm given a challenge of finding a simple way of communicating something deep so as to not overwhelm some of my disciples or students. However, in my case, the handicap of preaching or teaching in Spanish is what limits me.

I also spend a considerable amount of time with a few nationals who are barely literate, and who may not have listened to all the cutting edge sermons on an iPod, or even have access to the technology I have. As such, I need to communicate clearly and often cover things that may be basic and not "meaty," at least according to some of my friends if they were present and listening to my teaching. My experiences have helped me understand what Paul may have been saying here: "I have so much more to tell you but I can't yet."

Suffice it to say that also means that nothing Paul went on to teach in the rest of his letter is meant to be very profound. It's not deep stuff, but rather basic. Keep that in mind as we move forward in this chapter and come back to his letter to the Corinthians in later chapters.

> The Corinthians had gotten off track and began to try to operate in the spiritual gifts in the flesh or in their own effort.

The Purpose of the Gifts

First Corinthians 12 is a description of all of the spiritual gifts flowing together perfectly as intended within a community of believers. Not one gift is more important than the other, but all are needed for the "common good" (1 Corinthians 12:7). Paul then compares the gifts to a human body and how each part is necessary for the functioning of the whole person. The underlying issue that he was addressing was that the believers were not using the gifts properly and in an edifying manner. It appears that when they gathered, some were eating and getting drunk in front of those who may not have been able to contribute to their potluck type of gatherings. People were being neglected. Regarding the gifts themselves, some would stand and declare what appeared to be whole messages in tongues, without any interpretation, and people who were present didn't know what was going on. Then someone else would stand and try to outdo the last person.

As a result, the Corinthians had gotten off track and began to try to operate in the spiritual gifts in the flesh or in their own effort. They were not trying to build each other up, but it was almost like a contest to see who was the most spiritual. It was against this backdrop that Paul was setting things straight and getting back to the fundamentals. The Corinthians were not loving each other but were in competition with one another. Ironically, they missed the *purpose* behind the gifts. They had wound up using the gifts to show off how spiritual they thought *themselves* to be! The lack of love they were showing each other was the opposite purpose of the gifts, which serves as the backdrop as we reach the thirteenth chapter:

> *If I [can] speak in the tongues of men and [even] of angels, but have not love* (that reasoning, intentional, spiritual devotion such as is inspired by God's love for and in us), *I am only a noisy gong or a clanging cymbal.*
>
> *And if I have prophetic powers* (the gift of interpreting the divine will and purpose), *and understand all the secret truths and mysteries and possess all knowledge, and if I have [sufficient] faith so that*

I can remove mountains, but have not love (God's love in me) *I am nothing* (a useless nobody).

Even if I dole out all that I have [to the poor in providing] food, and if I surrender my body to be burned or in order that I may glory, but have not love (God's love in me), *I gain nothing.* (1 Corinthians 13:1-3, AMP)

Paul was telling them that it's one thing that they are able to speak in tongues and operate in the prophetic, but since they didn't have love, it meant nothing. God loves us and desires for us to love each other. In John 13:35 Jesus mentioned that people would know his disciples by their love. As a body of believers, we must love one another. If the Corinthians had love for one another, they would not have been competing to operate in the gifts. They demonstrated that they were still immature.

In the next few verses, Paul goes on to lay groundwork as to what this Christlike love looks like:

Love is patient and kind; love does not envy or boast; it is not arrogant or rude. It does not insist on its own way; it is not irritable or resentful; it does not rejoice at wrongdoing, but rejoices with the truth. Love bears all things, believes all things, hopes all things, endures all things. (1 Corinthians 13:4-7)

Within this context, we read the rest of the chapter in view of the progression through Paul's letter to the Corinthians up until this point. If we read this passage plainly, without any external notions or preunderstanding imposed on the text, it becomes difficult to reach an idea that Paul was referring to the canon of Scripture in his letter at this point. That's to say, Paul is not talking about all the books of the Bible being compiled at some time. Love is the context and backdrop, not theology or church order itself.

> *Love never fails [never fades out or becomes obsolete or comes to an end]. As for prophecy (the gift of interpreting the divine will and purpose), it will be fulfilled and pass away; as for tongues, they will be destroyed and cease; as for knowledge, it will pass away [it will lose its value and be superseded by truth].*
>
> *For our knowledge is fragmentary (incomplete and imperfect), and our prophecy (our teaching) is fragmentary (incomplete and imperfect).*
>
> *But when the complete and perfect (total) comes, the incomplete and imperfect will vanish away (become antiquated, void, and superseded).* (1 Corinthians 13:8-10, AMP)

God intends the Scriptures to work in tandem with his people revealing who he is. We need both in order to know him—one doesn't supersede the other.

It is at this point that Paul is seeking to show that these gifts are part of a greater whole, with everybody having a part to play in building up the whole church (1 Corinthians 14:26). The specific reason we have fellowship is to love one another and contribute to the revelation of Jesus in each of our hearts and to build one another up in edification. Therefore, if we are not using the gifts in love they are not actually useful and they are rendered ineffective. We are like a sounding gong or a clanging cymbal.

But as we mature as believers and a body of Christ, we are going to no longer see in part, but see as a whole, putting away childish things and growing into maturity. In this current age, we get prophetic glimpses of Jesus from his Word, his Spirit, and his people, but one day we will see him face to face for ourselves. God intends the Scriptures to work in tandem with his people revealing who he is. We need both in order to know him—one doesn't supersede the other.

How People's Bias Affects Their Reading of the Text

When I lived in the Netherlands during my mid-twenties, I remember my friend Dan was leading a young adult Bible study and we'd experiment with this passage. We'd ask newer believers who had never previously heard of cessationism what they thought this passage was talking about. I have also done the same on occasions with Peruvians now that I live in South America. The result has often been predictable. They'd usually never guess this meant anything other than what Paul plainly says. I have yet to see someone come to the conclusion that the "perfect" is referring to Scripture canon being completed without having been taught this by someone else first. One does not seem to reach this interpretation on his or her own.

Dr. Stephen Crosby agrees that cessationism is something that's taught and not learned from the Scriptures:

> If the Bible was given to an individual with no Christian or biblical exposure whatsoever and the person

read it, the individual would not be a Cessationist as a result of the reading. Cessationism is inferential. It must be taught. It is a learned or acquired hermeneutic, not Scripture's self-testimony.[1]

Reformed charismatic theologian R. T. Kendall also holds this view, writing:

> Some take the "perfect" to be the Bible—when the church finally agreed upon the exact canon of Scripture. Whereas I too agree that the Bible is perfect, that is not what Paul means in 1 Corinthians 13. While it could be argued that the "perfect" refers to when we are in heaven, Paul surely meant "perfect love," which my book *Just Love* (a verse-by-verse exposition of 1 Corinthians 13) shows.[2]

> **Nowhere does the New Testament state that the gifts of the Holy Spirit are only for a certain period, then they were to cease, like proponents of the cessationist doctrine teach.**

What Paul has been basing his letter on, namely love, will one day soon be staring us in the face. The important thing is that we use the gifts in love, because on that day, when everything has been revealed, we won't need to prophesy about someone who at that time will be known fully. We will see him. Despite this, love will remain no matter whether or not these gifts are still in operation. It should also be noted that knowledge will not pass away, not even in heaven.

Therefore, the foundation is set for Paul's instructions on the operation of the spiritual enablements: we are to pursue love and earnestly desire the spiritual gifts. The apostle would not have gone on to address their use and encourage the Corinthian believers to earnestly desire them if he was expecting them to cease or if they would no longer be necessary at some point in the future. As established, the obvious flow of thought and motivation here is love.

Nowhere does the New Testament state that the gifts of the Holy Spirit are only for a certain period, then they were to cease, like proponents of the cessationist doctrine teach. It's likely that a key reason for the unbelief in this supernatural phenomenon is not based on anything stated in Scripture if one carefully reads the book of Acts, the rest of Paul's epistle to the Corinthians, and other satellite passages on the matter. These passages teach on the use of it in public gatherings, but nowhere imply or state that the use of the gifts—including but not limited to tongues—were only for the early church and not the church universal.

Jon Ruthven, who is a professor of systematic and practical theology at Regent University, states that if the function of the charismata determines their duration, then their edificatory, rather than simply evidential functions determine their continuation.[3] Until the fullness of the body of Christ is attained, every believer will need the fullness of the Spirit; therefore, we can't limit the experience and use of the charismatic gifts to the early church.

Dr. Crosby also casts doubt on the probability that the "perfect" Paul was referring to could have been the canon of Scripture:

No one would argue the verses refer to a time when charismatic manifestations will stop. The interpretive debate surrounds when. Some Cessationists argue the "perfect" refers to the completed canon of Scripture (about 90 AD) concurrent with the death of the last of the twelve original apostles.

One of the basic (and most vital) principles of biblical interpretation is original intent: a passage must be interpreted in a way the original author and hearers would have understood.

In 1 Cor. 13:8-10, there is no contextual mention of a New Testament canon of Scripture. That the verses apply to a yet future New Testament canon would have been totally alien to Paul and his hearers.

First Corinthians is an ad hoc personal letter likely written in reply to a previous correspondence to Paul from Corinth asking his advice on some issues. Paul was unaware that a future generation of theologians, centuries after his death, would canonize his letters as God-breathed Scripture. Time-bound interpretations and understandings that neither author nor hearer could have possessed must be rejected as inferentially reading into the text.

Paul may not have necessarily known he was writing something that would be included in Canon with his other epistles. This was just a letter being written to a church.[4]

> Just because the gifts, including speaking in tongues, had gone dormant, does not indicate it was originally what God intended.

In the closing of this chapter I'd like to end with a well-known story of church history that applies here. It is said that the theologian Thomas Aquinas once called on Pope Innocent II when the latter was counting out a large sum of money. The Pope remarked, "You see, Thomas, the church can no longer say, 'Silver and gold have I none.'" Aquinas replied, "True, holy father, but neither can she now say, 'Rise and walk.'"

The fact that historically the church at the time was no longer lacking in finances and seemingly able to give to any who asked was not necessarily indicative of the presence of God if, likewise, they could no longer perform a miracle in his name. Just because it had happened doesn't mean it was supposed to be that way. Likewise, over the centuries that followed the early church's inauguration, just because the gifts, including speaking in tongues, had gone dormant, does not indicate it was originally what God intended.

Notes

1. Stephen R. Crosby, *Your Empowered Inheritance: Now!* (Stephanos Ministries), 176.

2. R.T. Kendall, *Holy Fire: A Balanced, Biblical Look at the Holy Spirit's Work in Our Lives* (Charisma House), Location 2301, Kindle.

3.   Jon Ruthven, On the Cessation of the Charismata: The Protestant Polemic on Post-Biblical Miracles http://hopefaithprayer.com/word-of-faith/on-the-cessation-of-the-charismata/ (accessed on November 18, 2013).

4.   Stephen R. Crosby, *Your Empowered Inheritance: Now!* (Stephanos Ministries), 137.

Chapter 7

Tongues Are Not for Everyone—They're Just One of the Many Gifts

So far we've clarified that Pentecostals don't typically believe that you're not saved unless you speak in tongues. We've established that the baptism in the Holy Spirit is a separate experience from salvation and not included in it. Maybe you didn't believe those unscriptural misconceptions, and maybe you don't struggle with the idea that tongues are for today. You may be saying to yourself, "Steve, I totally believe they're for today. I just don't believe there's a one-size-fits-all aspect to it. They're one of the gifts, but they're not for everybody." That's where I'd like to encourage you to stop missing out on something if you've never experienced this gift yourself.

Let's revisit the occurrences in the book of Acts when the believers in the early church received the baptism in the Holy

Spirit for the first time, and when the spiritual gifts were introduced into the body of Christ. Since we already spent time looking at the four key moments in Luke's record when Spirit baptism happened, I won't be too repetitive here. We'll merely approach a few texts again but with a different emphasis.

> *When the day of Pentecost arrived, they were all together in one place. And suddenly there came from heaven a sound like a mighty rushing wind, and it filled the entire house where they were sitting. And divided tongues as of fire appeared to them and rested on* **each one of them.** *And they were* **all filled** *with the Holy Spirit and* **began to speak in other tongues** *as the Spirit gave them utterance.* (Acts 2:1-4)

Notice here, the first time this event is documented in the Scriptures, what does it mention? Reread the above passage carefully and try not to read into it what it doesn't actually say.

Okay, I'll give you a hint.

The *entire* house they were in had a sound in it, and each believer had what appeared to be a tongue of fire on his or her head. The text *does not* say the Holy Spirit distributed a tongue of fire on *some* of their heads as he willed, but that the tongue appeared to rest on *each one of them*. In the very next sentence we read that they *all* were filled and began to speak with other tongues. If the gift of speaking in tongues is just one of the several gifts to be expected, and is not to be given special attention, then how come Luke didn't write, "When the Holy Spirit came on them, the gift of healing manifested and people got out of wheelchairs"?

I know, it's because they didn't have wheelchairs back then.

Okay, better example. How come it doesn't say, "Then people got up and started prophesying things that would happen one day in the future"? There's no mention of anything else other than a tongue that looked like a flame—or a flame that looked like a tongue—on each of their heads, and that these all spoke as the Holy Spirit gave them utterance. We see no other manifestation or gift of the Holy Spirit mentioned here on the inaugural day of the Holy Spirit's power other than speaking in tongues.

> The text *does not* say the Holy Spirit distributed a tongue of fire on *some* of their heads as he willed, but that the tongue appeared to rest on *each one of them*.

The Samaritans Believe Philip's Gospel

As we made note of in a previous chapter, in Acts 8 John and Peter later visited the believers who had accepted the gospel message in Samaria. They came later and laid hands on them to receive the Holy Spirit, possibly weeks after they'd converted or received salvation. The gift of tongues is not mentioned once here, but let's take a look at the text carefully and see something interesting:

> *But there was a man named Simon, who had previously practiced magic in the city and amazed the people of Samaria, saying that he himself was somebody great. They all paid attention to him, from the least to the greatest, saying, "This man is the power*

*of God that is called Great." And they paid attention to him because for a long time he had amazed them with his magic. But when they believed Philip as he preached good news about the kingdom of God and the name of Jesus Christ, they were baptized, both men and women. Even Simon himself believed, and after being baptized he continued with Philip. **And seeing signs and great miracles performed, he was amazed**.* (Acts 8:8-13)

In Philip's gospel presentation it's obvious there were miracles performed that amazed Simon, a man who without the power of the true living God was already able to perform "miracles." Stuff was going on that amazed even him, the man the people of Samaria nicknamed "the power of God that is called Great." This is all taking place before John and Peter had arrived to lay hands on all of them so they too could receive the Holy Spirit.

Now remember, we receive the Holy Spirit the moment we're born again and accept Jesus Christ as our Savior and Lord. But the phraseology or semantics here show that they still had not yet received something until John and Peter came and laid their hands on them.

Now when Simon saw that the Spirit was given through the laying on of the apostles' hands, he offered them money, saying, "Give me this power also, so that anyone on whom I lay my hands may receive the Holy Spirit." (Acts 8:18-19)

I've heard people say that Peter's admonition a few verses later, that Simon's heart was not right before the Lord (Acts

8:21-23) and he was in the gall of iniquity, indicates he was not a believer yet and therefore didn't know any better. But this is improbable since verse 13 already mentions that he believed Philip's preaching with the signs and wonders that amazed the people. However, one thing we do know for certain is that something different was happening when the people received the Holy Spirit, something that could verifiably indicate for observers, like Simon, that the Holy Spirit had come on those whom John and Peter laid hands on, something different than the signs and miracles Philip had performed. Therefore, it's highly unlikely that the verifiable signal that the believers in Samaria were getting filled with the Holy Spirit was something that they had already seen or experienced before hands were laid on them.

I won't be dogmatic about it, since the Scriptures don't specifically say what Simon saw in particular when people received the Holy Spirit, but there clearly was something that outwardly signaled to the rest of the people that it had happened. Judging from the pattern so far in Acts 2, and what we'll see two more times in subsequent chapters, it was very likely glossolalia.

The Gentiles at Cornelius's House

A couple of chapters later, Peter was given a vision and told to go to the house of Cornelius and share the gospel with him. When he did, there were evidences and signs that they too had received the Holy Spirit just like the Jewish believers had previously:

> *While Peter was still saying these things, the Holy Spirit fell on all who heard the word. And the believers from among the circumcised who had come with Peter were amazed, because the gift of the Holy Spirit*

*was poured out even on the Gentiles. **For they were hearing them speaking in tongues** and extolling God. Then Peter declared, "Can anyone withhold water for baptizing these people, who have **received the Holy Spirit just as we have?**"* (Acts 10:44-47)

It's clear that those present with Peter, those "among the circumcised who had come," were able to observe that the Gentile believers had also received the Holy Spirit just as they had previously. How did they know this? There was outward evidence of "them speaking in tongues and extolling God." Not only did they receive the Holy Spirit, but it would appear that they received him in a very similar way, except with no mention of a mighty rushing wind or tongues of fire on their heads. Mention is made that they were speaking things that signaled to those present that the same thing had happened to them had happened to the others who had also received.

Paul and John's Disciples at Ephesus

Many years after this event, denoted by nine chapters of narrative, we then read the account of Paul encountering disciples of John the Baptizer. As we already looked at previously, Paul asked them if they had received the Holy Spirit upon believing, and they answered in the negative, not even knowing there was such a Holy Spirit.

> *On hearing this, they were baptized in the name of the Lord Jesus. And **when Paul had laid his hands on them, the Holy Spirit came on them, and they began speaking in tongues and prophesying.** There were about twelve men in all.* (Acts 19:5-6)

In this encounter, after Paul laid his hands on John's disciples, the text states that they began to speak prophetic utterances and glossolalia. If we look at each instance believers receive the Holy Spirit in the book of Acts, the overwhelming majority of times it's accompanied with speaking in tongues as summarized in the figure below.

> **The purpose of speaking in tongues is not to indicate that the person is now better or more mature or filled with more power then a believer who doesn't, or who hasn't yet spoken in tongues.**

Figure 1: Reception of the Holy Spirit in Acts

Text	Persons	Occurrence
Acts 2:1-4	The disciples	Glossolalia and prophetic utterance
Acts 8:8-13	The Samaritans	None recorded
Acts 10:44-47	The Gentiles at Cornelius's house	Glossolalia
Acts 19:1-6	The disciples of John the Baptist	Glossolalia and prophetic utterance

We see that in each instance of Spirit baptism or reception of the Holy Spirit recorded in the book of Acts, prophetic utterance or glossolalia or both occurred. No other spiritual gift is documented with the baptism in the Holy Spirit.

The purpose of speaking in tongues as a signal or evidence of receiving the baptism of the Holy Spirit is not to indicate that the person doing the speaking in tongues is now better or more mature or filled with more power then a believer who doesn't, or who hasn't yet spoken in tongues. I liken it to placing a key in the ignition of a car. Doing so does nothing other than turning the car on. You hear the engine starting and maybe smoke begins to come out from the exhaust pipe. You don't stop there and say, "Yes, I've got a car that makes noise!" but you go and actually drive it somewhere. The engine making a noise is a signal, or evidence, that the engine works and that you can go ahead and take it for a spin.

Speaking in tongues in this sense is a mere indication that the engine is now turned on to a new level than when the car was parked. Once that contact is made from the key into the car's ignition and turned correctly, something is ignited. It's the same when the Holy Spirit comes on someone for the first time in this post-conversion way.

But you don't stop there. The point of the baptism in power is to be a witness in power and bring the gospel with signs and wonders that follow to a lost and dying world around you (Mark 16:15-18). If someone got excited that their car made noises every time they put the key in the ignition, I wouldn't be too impressed or excited with them. But if they could take me for a ride on the Autobahn in Germany or cruise at fast speeds around a motor speedway, that would be an even better evidence of the power their car contains.

Likewise, don't be impressed just because someone has the ability to speak in tongues. Pay attention to what type of powerful witness his or her life is. The same way you want a car that works, likewise you don't want to just speak in tongues. You want to be a witness for Christ with power.

In the closing of this chapter, I'd like to remind you that "gift" is a translation of the Greek word *charisma*, which means grace, favor, or kindness. A superior shows charisma or favor to his or her inferior. It is used when God gives something good to men. Therefore, if it is for one, then it's for all. Just receive it and honor the Lord by using it a lot.

Chapter 8

Speaking in Tongues Is the Least of the Gifts

*S*ome readers may find it peculiar that I'm including a chapter on the order in which the apostle Paul lists the spiritual gifts. When I began writing this book, the most visited post on my blog through search engines was for phrases like "speaking in tongues is the least of the gifts," or that "Paul lists tongues last," and other variations of this query. Clearly, there are a lot of people searching Google to find out information on this subject. This indicates that this is obviously something in need of much clarity in the body of Christ today. Even though I will spend less time on this particular lie than the others, I probably hear this one the most often.

> This alone does not indicate the gifts are listed in a descending ranking order any more than page numbers in a book would indicate the content on those pages is more important if it's written chronologically first to last.

Why Do You Place Such an Overemphasis on Speaking in Tongues?

Every so often I hear an objector refer to this practice as the "lesser" gift or "least of the gifts," when there is in fact no such Scripture stating that tongues is the least of the gifts. Nor are there any indications that Paul's list of spiritual gifts is ordered in any kind of importance. This is especially obvious when we consider that at other times when Paul makes lists, he doesn't list things in the same order, making me conclude it was of no importance to Paul's thinking. From asking friends who understand New Testament Greek better than I do, it becomes clear that the order of Paul's list of gifts here is in contradiction to the order he lists in other places in the Scriptures.

> *And God has appointed in the church first apostles, second prophets, third teachers, then miracles, then gifts of healing, helping, administrating, and various kinds of tongues. Are all apostles? Are all prophets? Are all teachers? Do all work miracles? Do all possess gifts of healing? Do all speak with tongues? Do all interpret? But earnestly desire the higher gifts.*
> (1 Corinthians 12:28-31)

"But Steve, Paul uses indicators here, like first, second, thirdly, etc.... Clearly this is indicative of importance and order." In his book *Reimagining Church*, Frank Viola tackles this passage from a standpoint of reading hierarchy into the text where there is none:

> Again, this question is indicative of our penchant for reading Scripture with the tainted spectacles of human hierarchy. It's a peculiarly Western foible to

insist that every relationship be conceived in terms of a one-up/one-down hierarchical mode. Thus whenever we see an ordered list in the New Testament (like 1 Corinthians 12:28) we can't seem to help ourselves from connecting the dots of hierarchy.[1]

The context Viola is dealing with in this portion of Scripture is that of spiritual authority and covering, as noted by the first items on the list being apostles, then prophets. But I feel it applies here since the text is about building the church. Viola states:

A more natural reading of this passage understands the ordering to reflect a logical priority rather than a hierarchical one. In other words, the order reflects the greater gifting with respect to church building. This interpretation meshes nicely with the immediate context in which it appears. (1 Cor. 12,13,14)[2]

Since apostles lay the foundation of a church, they're listed first in a chronological perspective, not necessarily one of importance, in the work of church building. Yet, even though the apostles are listed first in building a church, they're viewed as last in the eyes of the world (Matthew 20:16; 1 Corinthians 4:9). This alone does not indicate these are listed in a descending ranking order any more than page numbers in a book would indicate the content on those pages is more important if it's written chronologically first to last.

Let's look at other examples of lists Paul makes and ponder whether or not the order of things mentioned is from most important to least important, as some would have us believe about the order of the gifts Paul lists in 1 Corinthians 12. In Romans, Paul writes:

For as in one body we have many members, and the members do not all have the same function, so we, though many, are one body in Christ, and individually members one of another. Having gifts that differ according to the grace given to us, let us use them: if prophecy, in proportion to our faith; if service, in our serving; the one who teaches, in his teaching; the one who exhorts, in his exhortation; the one who contributes, in generosity; the one who leads, with zeal; the one who does acts of mercy, with cheerfulness. (Romans 12:4-10)

Then in Ephesians Paul makes another list:

And he gave the apostles, the prophets, the evangelists, the shepherds and teachers, to equip the saints for the work of ministry, for building up the body of Christ, until we all attain to the unity of the faith and of the knowledge of the Son of God, to mature manhood, to the measure of the stature of the fullness of Christ, so that we may no longer be children, tossed to and fro by the waves and carried about by every wind of doctrine, by human cunning, by craftiness in deceitful schemes. (Ephesians 4:11-14)

> This function of the gift of tongues *in a corporate setting* is not something everybody will function in.

In both of these passages of Scripture, in comparison to the "list" in 1 Corinthians 12, the apostle Paul lists some things in a different order between these lists, and he orders some things inconsistently—that's to say, he places some things in one list and not in another or others that can be found elsewhere in the New Testament.

If we compare the ministry gifts list in Ephesians 4 to 1 Corinthians 12, we'll notice that both begin with apostles and prophets. But I'm persuaded that, since Paul begins both lists in Ephesians and Corinthians the same way, it's possible he's referring more to offices or roles in the body of Christ than gifts per se.

"Steve, you're just getting hung up on semantics!" you may be thinking. You'd be right if I didn't clarify what I mean. It's more likely Paul is talking about the individuals themselves in a public gathering who will operate in the functions mentioned here in chapter 12 of his letter to the Corinthians. Is everybody going to be apostolic in nature? Of course not. Are all prophets? No. Some are, some aren't. Likewise, this function of the gift of tongues *in a corporate setting* is not something everybody will function in. Likewise, not everybody will function in the role of interpretation of the tongue either. It's a matter that can be exacerbated if we don't distinguish in chapters 12–14 when Paul is referring to praying in a personal prayer language versus when he is referring to the roles the believers take on in building up the church family (and not building up the individual).

The thought here toward greater gifting is in the context of building up the church body. Some plant, such as an apostle does, and some water, such as a teacher does (1 Corinthians 3:6). To use the building and edification metaphor, this does not indicate a pecking order of some kind with regard to tools used to build up the church. All are useful and given to the collection of believers in diverse ways as the Spirit sees fit.

> **Have you ever heard a believer suggest "orgies" are a "lesser sin" because Paul mentions them last in that list? I didn't think so.**

Inconsistency in Approach

I know very few people who use this descending ranking order approach with other lists of Paul's elsewhere in the New Testament, such as lists of sins that will keep individuals from inheriting the kingdom of God.

> *Now the works of the flesh are evident: sexual immorality, impurity, sensuality, idolatry, sorcery, enmity, strife, jealousy, fits of anger, rivalries, dissensions, divisions, envy, drunkenness, orgies, and things like these. I warn you, as I warned you before, that those who do such things will not inherit the kingdom of God.* (Galatians 5:19-21)

The last sin mentioned that will prevent a person from entering the kingdom of God, according to this list, is orgies and "things like these." Have you ever heard a believer suggest "orgies" are a "lesser sin" because Paul mentions them last in that list? I didn't think so.

Then Paul goes on to talk about the fruit the Spirit produces within God's people: "But the fruit of the Spirit is love, joy, peace, patience, kindness, goodness, faithfulness, gentleness, self-control; against such things there is no law" (Galatians 5:22-23). Have you ever heard a believer try telling you that the order the fruit of the Spirit is listed in is from most important to least important? Have you ever heard anybody state that self-control is not important, or that it's the least important fruit of the Spirit because it's mentioned last? I didn't think so.

To be consistent, cessationists would need to admit that the *interpretation* of tongues is not as important as tongues speaking itself—according to this "list"—because it is listed below "tongues." Also, the message of wisdom and knowledge "ranks" first and second in Paul's alleged list, when they are actually "prophecy," just as tongues with interpretation is listed. When cessationists say that the gift of tongues is not very important, they are saying that prophesying is not important either. In Romans 12, prophecy is the first gift listed, ahead of serving and teaching. It becomes obvious the problem so-called "ranking" becomes when we compare Scripture with Scripture.

In First Corinthians 12:28-31 the cessationist approach results in confusion since only the first three gifts seem to be listed in a ranking order, with all the other gifts lumped together as a general fourth. Notice that the gifts of miracles and healings are listed above the gifts of administrative leadership. I've never heard a cessationist admit or teach that administration is of little importance due to its ranking in Paul's other list over in Romans.

If we follow this "least gift" approach to its natural conclusion and use it consistently, then those who are in leadership positions or administration are not as important as those who help them—"those able to help others"—because they are lower on the list as well. The "best gifts," according to Paul in these chapters, are "prophecy" and "interpretation." But, of course, in chapter 13 we see that "love" is considered the most important.

> **It becomes obvious the problem so-called "ranking" becomes when we compare Scripture with Scripture.**

It should be mentioned again that Paul was writing to the Corinthians concerning their time of fellowship, or as we could say, their church services. Therefore, for these gatherings it would appear that interpretation and prophecy are the most important gifts, with "apostles" and "prophets" being the most important *offices* or roles. Yet, most of the individuals I've come across would also rule out the importance of apostles and prophets and do hermeneutical acrobatics so as to explain away the use of apostles and prophets in the contemporary church.

I've also had cessationist friends and colleagues point out to me that if we look at the only other time Paul seems to mention the spiritual gifts, which is in his letter to the Romans, then we should notice tongues is not listed there at all. Ironically enough, it escapes their notice that Paul doesn't mention pastoring either! Do cessationists really believe that pastoring is not important because it is not on that particular list? Can you see how this falls apart on itself if we try applying this logic all over the place whenever Paul mentions *anything* in his letters that appears to be in a specific order?

This list stuff seems to be a matter of picking and choosing based on denominational stances or personal convictions more than Scripture itself. Does the exclusion of something in Paul's lists denote its lack of significance if we're going to insist that the order of what's included in the list is of importance? One can't have it both ways! The question of how important or unimportant tongues are should really be a moot point for any discussion on the matter since none of us qualify to pass judgment on what the Holy Spirit does.

And to play with the absurdity of this "list" stuff even further, the Bible also says that the first shall be last and the last shall be first (in the context of the parable of the vineyard workers in Matthew 20:16). Contextually, that is not talking about earthly role reversals in heaven or that the last person to enter into the kingdom will be as the first one to enter. We don't place importance in the order in this regard, but if we did, we would see that the role Paul mentioned first, the apostle, is also mentioned elsewhere as last. How does this work? Again, we can't have it both ways when it suits our doctrinal convenience.

In conclusion, the only distinction Paul makes is that the gifts that are the most "efficient" for the community, which have the broadest benefit, and which would be corporate over individual gifts are to be preferred in a corporate setting. This does not indicate or imply that any of the gifts themselves are more important than any other just because of the order they are listed. If it did, then Paul would have been consistent in the way he ordered things in his list. The reader is invited to compare Galatians 5:16-25, Colossians 3:5-9, and Ephesians 5:1-16.

Believers who espouse this view should be challenged to hold to it consistently in all passages that have lists. We easily fall into error when we interpret the order the gifts are referred to as having any special importance. Maybe the truth of the matter is that some of us are the ones deciding which gifts are the most important? Truly, no gift from God is unimportant, even if it does come last on a list.

Notes

1. Frank Viola, *Reimagining Church* (David C. Cook Publications), Location 3736, Kindle.

2. Ibid., location 3736.

Chapter 9

Legitimate Tongues Require an Interpretation

In the first section of this book I mentioned a charismatic church outside of my hometown that a certain Bible college student told me to stay away from. He's the one who told me they hypnotize you by worshiping for hours until you've let your defenses down and will believe anything that's preached. As I mentioned previously, I'd usually just ask Pentecostal Bible college students if they really believed and practiced what I was told. For that same reason, on one of the nights I attended a Sunday evening service, I went with a friend of mine who started to attend the same Brethren Bible college the following year. This particular friend, whom I'll name Chris, was way more open to charismatic stuff than most of his classmates, but still had some similar confusion as I did at the time.

During the singing, some of the leaders remained on the platform during the worship, which was sometimes spontaneous. At one point the leaders started guiding the congregation through the use of some of the spiritual gifts, particularly tongues with interpretation, and prophecy. The main pastor stated that someone present had a tongue, and someone else had an interpretation. Immediately after that, someone present shouted out something that was a prophetic declaration. To my shock, the pastor interrupted him and said, "Brother, now is not the time to give prophetic words, please hold off on that for a moment." It seemed odd to me at the time that someone could just turn on and off the prophetic, so you can imagine I felt very similar with the gift of speaking in tongues.

> We have a lot of confusion concerning when exactly the gift of tongues requires an interpretation and when it wouldn't because many in the church unknowingly impose the same set of rules on each manifestation.

Someone had a declaration in tongues and moments later someone shared the interpretation of it. Afterward, when my friend Chris and the rest of our group we came with went to McDonalds for a bite to eat, I asked Chris what he thought of the service since I knew it was his first time attending. He told me he liked it, but that he especially liked how the pastors made sure there was an interpretation for the tongue, since "you aren't supposed to speak in tongues unless there's an interpreter." At the time, I would have been more inclined to agree with him, but that's when one of our friends who attended that fellowship explained to us that in a meeting, yes, but in private it wasn't necessary. I had little to contribute to this discussion that night and just listened as she made some good points.

The reason this misunderstanding in particular is so prevalent in the church today is because not much is taught about the diversities of tongues. We have a lot of confusion concerning when exactly the gift of tongues requires an interpretation and when it wouldn't because many in the church unknowingly impose the same set of rules on each manifestation.

I have heard different groupings and categorizations of tongues, but a case can be made in Scripture and from personal experience that there are up to four different manifestations of the gift of tongues. The Holy Spirit is the one who wills each of the diversifications, but there are differences that we can see in Scripture. We will look at them one at a time, but I must remind the reader that they are not listed here in any order of importance.

Tongues for interpretation (1 Corinthians 14:5). This manifestation of tongues is typically used or presented in a public gathering and usually accompanied by another believer, or oftentimes the same believer who gives the utterance in tongues. Simply put, it occurs when a message is given in an unknown language (tongue) and then interpreted. Most people already have a cursory knowledge that Paul told the Corinthians the following: "The one who prophesies is greater than the one who speaks in tongues, unless someone interprets, so that the church may be built up" (1 Corinthians 14:5). As such, if you ask non-charismatic believers, in certain circles, they'll tell you legitimate tongues are required to have an interpretation.

> **If we yield ourselves to God, he can lead us into intercession for those in our lives, such as family and friends, and even for those we don't know, such as leaders or figures we've never met.**

Tongues of deep intercessional groanings (Romans 8:26). This particular diversification of tongues may be manifested during deep travail or intercession as the Holy Spirit may lead the believer in prayer. It is one that the individual believer can move into and experience, whether in a public setting or not. But my understanding of Scripture leads me to conclude it can't typically be entered into at will. We can pray for something that may be close to groanings that we can't understand, and ask the Lord to reveal to us what we are praying in our own voice, and he may do just that.

We don't know how to pray in certain situations, but the Holy Spirit does. If we yield ourselves to God, he can lead us into intercession for those in our lives, such as family and friends, and even for those we don't know, such as leaders or figures we've never met. As we give into these leadings of intercession, the Lord answers our prayers since the Holy Spirit, who is a member of the holy Trinity, motivates them. If you are willing to allow the Lord to use you in this way, he will. However, like the corporate gift of tongues and interpretation, a believer can't simply enter into this type of intercession just any time he or she wants. We can come to the throne of God boldly in our prayer time with an honest heart and tell the Lord we feel burdened about a situation or circumstance, and he may lead us in intercession.

Tongues as a sign to the unbeliever (1 Corinthians 14:22). This is what happened on the day of Pentecost in Acts 2. This diversification occurs when the Holy Spirit bypasses or transcends the believer's intellect and language barriers by enabling him or her to preach, testify, or teach about Christ using a known human language, which the believer doing the speaking has no prior knowledge of.

This is very similar to the first manifestation, and it is why some people group the two together when distinguishing the diversities of tongues. However, I'd distinguish it in that according to Scripture it doesn't seem to require an interpretation of the tongue spoken. This is further corroborated when we see that the listeners below all heard their own language being spoken, clearly indicating the tongues were understood by them, thereby removing the need for there to be an interpreter present.

An example of this type of manifestation would be when God enables a believer to speak in a known human tongue he or she has never spoken before, and there may or may not be any other believers present to give an interpretation. But let's just say a speaker of another language was present and heard their own native language being spoken and it convicted them or showed them God was real. This would be similar to tongues as a sign to unbelievers. I've never personally experienced this in my life or ministry yet, but I'm aware of it happening.

As a missionary to Peru and a fluent speaker of English, French, and Spanish, it would be absolutely no miracle whatsoever if I just stood up in a meeting and started speaking any of those three languages. There would be no way for God to be getting any glory in this situation because I already know these three languages and could speak French or Spanish at will.

English is my native language, in case that wasn't already obvious. But let's say I traveled to the jungle of Pucallpa, further inland than where I currently live in Peru. In this area there's a tribe of people called the Shipibos, and I'd need to travel with an interpreter who understands Spanish and Shipibo in order to help me communicate and preach effectively with the people in Pucallpa. It's highly improbable that I'd find an interpreter who spoke my native language of English.

Let's say, for illustrative purposes, that I travel there one week, and the first night I'm about to preach my interpreter gets kicked off a cliff by a goat and eaten alive by a pack of rabid wolverines that were gathered around the vat of toxic waste that he fell into. Hey, my hypothetical example is totally made up, so can't I be creative? So thanks to this rather unusual and unfortunate set of events, I'm now without an interpreter or translator, but yet I'm scheduled to preach meetings day and night for the next week. If the Holy Spirit then came on me in that moment, and enabled me to speak and preach in Shipibo, then that would be an example of this manifestation of tongues.

But let's go even further. In my made-up example an entire village witnessed my interpreter's death and heard through word of mouth that there was a gringo (or a tourist, basically) who was preaching in their language without ever having learned it. So they come out to the meeting, and in their own language I preach against sin, and I begin calling people out by name, and telling them what to repent of. I preach to someone else by their name, which is practically impossible to pronounce properly but somehow God enables me to do it, and I also speak to them about how God loves them and will provide for them. Someone else hears me preach about an affair they've been having for ten years that nobody knew about. As a result, this entire village repents of their sins and accepts Jesus as their Lord and Savior, and a revival breaks out. That would be a great example of the gift of tongues as a sign to the unbeliever.

> **The Lord can work however he wants in a meeting, but I do believe oftentimes we charismatics are not engaging in this type of tongue scripturally in many of our meetings.**

From my understanding this can be very similar to the first manifestation, but a scriptural case can be made that there are subtle differences. Some believers lump these four diversifications into just two categories: one for public use and the other for private. But a manifestation such as this one is only needed or necessary if there are unbelievers present. I've been in charismatic and Pentecostal meetings where there have been individuals who spoke in tongues and there was an interpreter, and, for all intents and purposes, I'm not sure how it was a sign to any unbelievers present. This is easier to determine if you're in a small meeting and personally know each person present.

At other times I've seen individuals share a tongue, and moments later interpret it themselves. Now, I'm not going to stand in the way if the Lord is truly doing that in our midst since his ways are not our ways, but wouldn't it make more sense that someone just has a prophetic word in that type of instance? Again, I'm just asking questions here. The Lord can work however he wants in a meeting, but I do believe oftentimes we charismatics are not engaging in this type of tongue scripturally in many of our meetings.

Tongues for personal edification (1 Corinthians 14:4). I listed this one last but by no means is it the least of the gifts (see what I did there?). I also want to spend considerable time on this one for the rest of the chapter since it is the most common one and perhaps the most unique of the four manifestations.

I'd define this diversification of tongues as the supernatural language the Holy Spirit prays through us that we can use to pray as little or however much we desire. This gift is available to all believers subsequent to the baptism in the Holy Spirit. Unlike the other three manifestations, as well as any of the other sign gifts Paul lists, this is the only one we can operate in at will.[1]

In John 14:17, Jesus said the Holy Spirit would be with us *and* in us. These are two different things. The Holy Spirit is with us *corporately* as a body of believers, and he's with the *individual* believer on the inside of us. He builds up the church and he builds up the individual believer as well.

> In the corporate setting the Holy Spirit distributes gifts freely as he sees fit, but we can seek after and desire to operate in some more than others for the benefit of the *rest of the church body*.

In 1 Corinthians 3:16, Paul tells the church at Corinth that they collectively, as a church, are the temple of the Holy Spirit. Not every Bible translation makes that obvious. The Amplified Bible brings out that the church is the temple of the Holy Spirit collectively, and the individual is the temple of the Holy Spirit individually. Compare this with 1 Corinthians 6:19, where we're told our *body* is a temple of the Holy Spirit.

This is also part of the reason why, when believers are baptized in the Holy Spirit sometime after their salvation experience, there are different varieties of the gift of tongues available to them. Each version of the Holy Spirit's "temple" has this phenomena manifested. In the corporate setting the Holy Spirit distributes gifts freely as he sees fit, but we can seek after and desire to operate in some more than others for the benefit of the *rest of the church body.* To one person the Holy Spirit can distribute the corporate version of the gift of tongues, and another believer the interpretation in a public setting. It's true—not every believer has the *corporate* version of the gift of tongues. This is what I am convinced Paul was referring to—the local church setting—when he asked in 1 Corinthians 12:30, "Do all speak with tongues? Do all interpret?"

> As we yield to the Holy Spirit, he will build into us the revelation of everything Christ is in us, our hope and glory, and build into us the character of Christ.

However, every gift of the Holy Spirit that operates collectively in the body of Christ has an "individual" version of it for the believer. All may prophesy (1 Corinthians 14:31), all believers can speak in tongues (Mark 16:17), anyone who believes may lay hands on the sick (Mark 16:18), and so on.

Greek Definitions

In 1 Corinthians 14:4 Paul says that when someone speaks in an unknown tongue, the person speaking edifies himself. The word *edify* comes from the Greek work *oikodomeo,* which means to build a house or erect a building. It literally means to build upward, especially a skyline, or to top out a building or structure. An edifier is one who plans, designs, or constructs such edifices.

Oikodomeo has the same root as *oikodome*, which is similar in definition, but also emphasizes the act of one who promotes another's growth in Christian wisdom, piety, happiness, and holiness. Similarity, an *oikos*, not to be confused with the popular Greek yoghurt in North America, is literally an "extended family" or "household." Examples of *oikos* being used include Romans 16:3-5 and 1 Corinthians 16:19. It's also the name of the ministry my wife Lili and I are apart of in Chorrillos, Peru.

To keep with this motif of edification and building, when the believers got together to fellowship in the early church, it didn't resemble a large megachurch with only platform or pulpit ministries, such as the worship team doing all the ministering while eighty percent of the congregation sat and watched. More often than not, the local bodies of believers met in homes and in smaller groups (*oikos*).[2]

It follows then, that the more we understand what edification is, the more we understand this process of edifying ourselves, which literally has to do with renovating, improving, and strengthening the foundations of the "temple" of the Holy Spirit. As we yield to the Holy Spirit, he will build into us the revelation of everything Christ is in us, our hope and glory, and build into us the character of Christ.

That being said, there's the gift of tongues that edifies the *collective* temple of the Holy Spirit (1 Corinthians 14:5, 22), compared with the gift of tongues that edifies the *individual* temples of the Holy Spirit. It's my conviction, therefore, that of the four diversifications of tongues mentioned earlier, two types are for the benefit of the corporate gathering of believers, and one is accompanied by an interpretation, which could also include a natural language.

A helpful insight about tongues and interpretation comes from author James C. Davidson:

> Interpretation is the other half of a useful duo of gifts which bring messages from God to the church for its up-building. A message in tongues must be interpreted, otherwise it is not understood. But praying in tongues needs no interpretation. It is to God, not men. To the speaker in tongues, the difference between a message in tongues and prayer in tongues is as obvious as is the difference between preaching and praying to their speaker.[3]

The other two types of the gift of tongues are for the individual believer on a more personal level, for personal edification, or being built up in our faith. The interpretation comes in the form of revelation and/or strength in the believer's spirit. Every believer can benefit from this personal use of tongues, but its misunderstanding and the lack of familiar experience have hindered many evangelicals from entering into this realm of the Holy Spirit.

As mentioned, the gift for personal use is something that every believer can have following the baptism in the Holy Spirit.

Each instance the baptism in the Holy Spirit is talked about in Acts, the manifestation of other tongues accompanied it, and in Acts 19 prophecy did also. Both are revelation and edification tools that involve *speaking* something.

It's regarding this distinction that Paul says in church that "I would rather speak five words with my mind in order to instruct others, than ten thousand words in a tongue" (1 Corinthians 14:19). This does not negate the value of speaking in tongues privately for personal edification, but reinforces that when we come together as a gathering of believers for fellowship, it's beneficial to build up others, not just ourselves. Therefore, if glossolalia takes place in a meeting, it needs to adhere to the guidelines in the second or third manifestation we've listed, and under these conditions it makes sense then that there would need to be an interpreter.

Notes

1. We covered some of the following section at the conclusion on confession in my previous book, *Increase Your Faith*. Readers of that book will remember the rest of this chapter, but we merely touched on the importance of praying in tongues there in another context. I'd like to go more in-depth here and approach this from another angle.

2. This book won't dive further into organic or house churches for brevity and scope's sake. For further reading on that I'd encourage the reader to explore Frank Viola's book *Reimagining Church: Pursuing the Dream of Organic Christianity* that we've referred to already.

3. James C. Davidson, *The Happy Gift of Tongues,* Location 1211, Kindle.

Chapter 10

Tongues Are Only Known Languages

For years I've had nearly a 100 percent success rate when laying hands on believers to receive the baptism in the Holy Spirit, resulting in them speaking in tongues. I attribute this to spending time with people to find out exactly what their hang-ups are or what theological objections are holding them back from receiving. If I have to spend an hour with someone answering all his or her questions, then I will. If they are ready and only need to have someone lay hands on them, then I lay hands on them and give them space to speak in their new prayer language for a minute straight, give or take, pretending that I'm not even there.

I do these kinds of things to help people relax and not feel nervous about how silly they may sound. If people have spent years believing wrong things about speaking in tongues, I don't rush the process when they are finally open to receiving. I never ask them to repeat something I say, but I encourage and guide them in speaking out the syllables the Holy Spirit is inspiring them to say.[1]

At any rate, the reason I say I've had *nearly* a 100 percent success rate, instead of a *full* success rate, is because I will bear with each person individually, if at all possible, removing every barrier they may have. I don't like getting up in front of a crowd or speaking into a microphone and merely praying over an audience full of people seeking this experience because, more often than not, this leads to people believing they've received something from God—which they have! However, since in that scenario they might not know how to release their new prayer language, it's easy for them to walk away believing that they've received the baptism in the Holy Spirit without speaking in tongues, which they might conclude as unnecessary in the use of this gift. For this reason I prefer one-to-one or small group settings for helping solve whatever someone's problem is.

Another reason my "success rate" is not fully 100 percent is because my Ukrainian friend named Dima brings my average down.

> I don't like getting up in front of a crowd or speaking into a microphone and merely praying over an audience full of people seeking this experience.

God's Sense of Humor

Before you continue reading, you need to know that I've gotten permission from my friend Dima and his wife to write about his story in this book, and offered to change his name to something else if he was worried of what I might share with the millions of people who are going to be reading this. Okay, maybe just thousands of people who are going to read this. For respect of their privacy only first names are used and nothing more.

I first met Dima around Rotterdam, the Netherlands, in early 2007 when I was living there as a missionary. Mutual friends introduced us, as he was also a non-Dutch living in the Netherlands, and we hit off a friendship right away. In little time at all I'd find myself at his and his wife's (Tanya) apartment on the other side of Rotterdam on a near weekly basis. He had a strong gift for teaching creationism and Genesis and eventually I got to help him with organizing and setting up a seminar in one of the local colleges with another young man who was looking to do that type of outreach on his campus.

Over time I started having dinner and attending an Alpha Course based Bible study at Dima and Tanya's apartment every Wednesday night. When it was over I'd spend *at least* an hour answering Dima's concerns and objections about the baptism in the Holy Spirit and speaking in tongues. Sometimes I felt like we were going in circles and answering the same questions. But fortunately, I knew Dima was serious and seeking, wanting to have answers to his concerns and not just arguing for the sake of arguing. He was no fool and was very knowledgeable in the Scriptures, and in answering his questions I feel like it sharpened my understanding of why I believe the Scriptures and speaking in tongues the way I do. Some of the things I learned during those months I've elaborated on in this book.

His wife once encouraged me that spending all those hours week after week was not a waste of time, and that her husband was the same with creationism at first. She told me he needed answers to his questions and what looked like "contradictions" in the Scriptures. But she assured me that once he got a hold of it he'd run with it and become an excellent apologist for the things of the Holy Spirit, just like he had done with creationism. I assumed the same type of passion was going to take place only if I exercised patience and gave him all the time he needed with the whole speaking in tongues thing.

One Wednesday night Dima told me he'd come the next Saturday to the Firehouse, which was the name of the cafe I was a part of as a missionary. He told me he believed he'd get filled with the Holy Spirit on that night. I tried encouraging him that he didn't have to wait until Saturday and could be filled right then, but ultimately there was no talking him out of it. He was certain this upcoming Saturday night was the night, so I acquiesced.

Saturday night came, and Dima and Tanya both came to the Firehouse. To avoid being a distraction to the others present, we went downstairs into the basement where my leader Frank, my roommate Joel, and a few others present, went to lay hands on Dima and pray for him to receive.

We prayed.

And prayed.

And just like on other occasions, nothing seemed to be happening.

Eventually people disappeared like I imagine they did when Jesus told whoever was without sin that they should cast the first stone at the woman who was caught in adultery. Dima and I wound up continuing in conversation on one of the bright yellow couches upstairs after many people had left for the night.

Eventually closing time came around and everybody left and it was just us still sitting there. I stayed with Dima since I had one of the keys to the building, and agreed with my leader that I'd lock up when we left. Eventually 11:00 p.m. came around and I realized that my 100 percent streak of getting people to speak in tongues was going to come to an end as I was very tired and this just did not seem to happen that night. Dima was cool with it as well since he needed to get back home. He had a small subway ride ahead of him whereas I only lived blocks away. But the confusion he shared with me for why he didn't receive was contagious, as I also didn't understand what the Lord was doing with this delay.

I don't recall how many weeks passed, but sometime later Benny Hinn was doing a crusade in Rotterdam and Dima and his wife both went to it. I remember knowing about it but for whatever reason not attending. The next time I saw Dima, he had a smile from ear to ear and told me he had *finally* gotten baptized in the Holy Spirit and was now speaking in tongues. I was not just relieved because of excitement that he received this life-changing spiritual gift and I knew he'd benefit from it, but in a way I had started to get worried it was never going to happen. Whether he had already been baptized in the Holy Spirit on another occasion prior to the first time he had ever spoken in tongues is up to interpretation, but at any rate he was satisfied he had gotten what he was seeking after.

He told me that at the crusade, there was a call for people to go forward and receive prayer for something, of which I now forget. Dima told me he went forward and as he stepped into the aisle, he fell to the ground. He described it as getting knocked over by the Holy Spirit. When he got up, he was then speaking in tongues. He shared this news with me believing I'd be excited for him. And I was. But I was also a little irked at God as I thought of the accumulated hours upon hours I'd spent with Dima over the previous months answering all his objections and praying for him. And now God saw fit to just knock him to the ground and give it to him?

Not funny, God. Not funny at all.

Experience *never* trumps the Word of God.

Googling Your Glossolalia?

At any rate, in the fall of that year, I went back to Canada to raise funds for the upcoming year, and due to various circumstances and eventual change of God's direction for my life and ministry, I was delayed going back to Holland and would not see Dima again for some time. The next part of my life would make for another story, but suffice it to say that through divine providence I was in Holland in the summer of 2008, collecting my belongings because I was now preparing to move to Peru and begin a new mission there, where I still find myself to this day—and am loving it!

During that visit, Dima asked me if I had ever done something, which upon hearing him explain it I have to admit I had never even thought of or heard of someone doing before. He asked me if I had ever "googled" my tongues on the Internet to see if they were human languages. Of course I hadn't. Who would do such a flaky thing as that? But since I knew Dima was a solid believer, and would *never* consider him nutty, I heard him out and let him explain to me what he had discovered.

Now before I proceed to show and tell you what I learned from him that night, you need to understand I'm not trying to build a doctrine around the following. I'm just trying to show you something interesting. Experience *never* trumps the Word of God. This was merely an interesting discovery that hopefully will encourage you.

Shortly after Dima received the gift of tongues, his wife received it and found she was only able or inspired to say what seemed like three words. So she decided to log into Google and search for these words. She spelled the words in her native language of Russian, spelled in the way she thought she was pronouncing them. The first word she pasted, she discovered some kind of dictionary website which listed it as "truth" in Kazakhstan. This excited Dima since it was not just some random word, like "table" or "finger" or something, but a word he felt was directly related to the gospel—truth.

So Dima attempted the same thing and spelled out, in Russian, his first word into a Google search and the first result to show up was for a messianic Jewish site. To his excitement, this word he discovered was the Hebrew word for "spirit." In the Hebrew one of the names for Spirit of God is *Ruach Elohim*, and this first Google search had Dima encouraged that he and his wife may just have been saying actual words and phrases in known languages.

Dima found dictionary and baby name websites for each of the next ten words he searched for that he had spelled out in his journal, and it would detract too much if we investigated in more detail what I learned. When I had Dima on a later episode of my podcast to discuss the process he goes through for determining if something is actually a word, I thought the podcast discussion would be kooky and fun, but then a few months after I uploaded it to the Internet, thousands of people had downloaded it. To date it has been the most downloaded episode of the *Fire On Your Head* podcast until I posted one with authors S. J. Hill and Dr. Stephen Crosby on "The New Jezebel," and that episode beat its record for number of listens.

> **When believers build themselves up in the inner spirit through praying in the Holy Spirit, it's very possible they could be speaking known human languages.**

Only Known Languages?

I shared all that to say that I'm totally open to the idea that when believers build themselves up in the inner spirit through praying in the Holy Spirit, it's very possible they could be speaking known human languages. Some cessationists and others who don't believe in speaking in tongues often dismiss the gift for the believer with the objection that tongues are only known languages.

You'll notice I carefully worded the title of this section that tongues are *only* known languages. Obviously they can be other earthly languages, as we have Scripture to back this up. Paul mentions in 1 Corinthians 13:1 the ability for one to speak in tongues of men (known human languages) as well as tongues of angels (some form of spiritual languages), but neither one of which is of any importance without love. As well, it appears in Acts 2 when the Holy Spirit came on the believers in the upper room, the people down below from various other cultures and nations heard their own languages being spoken.

As a result, some take these passages of Scripture to incorrectly teach and state that every time one speaks in tongues, it must be a known human language or else it's not really tongues. They say that charismatics and Pentecostals who speak in tongues are not correctly doing it but are just babbling, talking gibberish, and as I've sometimes heard, hypnotizing themselves. The train of thought follows that when the Holy Spirit fell on the believers in Acts 2, they appear to have spoken in known languages. Allegedly the word in the Greek used elsewhere in the apostle Paul's writings indicates known human languages—so I'm told, but I'm not sure why it matters. The reason cited is because, as mentioned above, those present on the day of Pentecost heard the people in the upper room speaking their languages.

> **I do disagree with the interpretation and the emphasis given to the fact they were known languages as if this creates some kind of pin to hang one's theological hat on.**

Known Languages or Not? It Doesn't Really Matter

I don't disagree with any of the facts presented that yes, those present heard different languages being spoken that day, because that's what appears to have happened. However, I do disagree with the interpretation and the emphasis given to the fact they were known languages as if this creates some kind of pin to hang one's theological hat on. Let's take a look at that passage for a moment:

> Now there were dwelling in Jerusalem Jews, devout men from every nation under heaven. And at this sound the multitude came together, and they were bewildered, because **each one was hearing them speak** in his own language. And they were amazed and astonished, saying, "Are not all these who are speaking Galileans? And how is it that **we hear, each of us in his own native language?** Parthians and Medes and Elamites and residents of Mesopotamia, Judea and Cappadocia, Pontus and Asia, Phrygia and Pamphylia, Egypt and the parts of Libya belonging to Cyrene, and visitors from Rome, both Jews and proselytes, Cretans and Arabians— we hear them telling in our own tongues the mighty works of God." And all were amazed and perplexed, saying to one another, "What does this mean?" But others mocking said, "They are filled with new wine." (Acts 2:5-13)

I have a hard time believing the people in the upper room were necessarily speaking known languages. Or what if they were? That doesn't invalidate how in 1 Corinthians 13 Paul mentions speaking in the tongues of men *and* of angels. Just think about the probability and likelihood of being able to understand your own language being spoken when coming across approximately twelve people gathered in a room above you each speaking a different language. If they all spoke one at a time, then yes, you could understand what they said. But it would be a remarkable feat if you were able to understand *one* language in particular emerging out of the twelve if they were all praying or worshiping at the same time out loud.

Do you really think someone is capable of clearly and decisively distinguishing their own language from the crowd if there were a hundred and twenty people speaking at the same time in different languages? Even more unlikely! That's why this miracle is even more remarkable than just people speaking new languages they had never previously spoken. It's highly doubtful they were speaking one at a time, since as we see there were probably one hundred and twenty individuals there. And if that many people were to pray one at a time, I'm not so sure it would still be early in the morning (Acts 2:15).

The miracle that happened at Pentecost was not necessarily that one was happening in what was being *spoken*, but a miracle in what was being *heard* by those from the other regions down below the upper room. Here's why I know that: this has happened before in Scripture where a group of people witnessed the same thing but heard something different:

> *"Father, glorify your name." Then a voice came from heaven: "I have glorified it, and I will glorify it again." The crowd that stood there and heard it said it had thundered. Others said, "An angel has spoken to him." Jesus answered, "This voice has come for your sake, not mine."* (John 12:28-30)

When a voice spoke from heaven glorifying Jesus, the people present heard conflicting things, but that's the point: some people's ears were open to hear thunder; at the same time, others were open to hearing the sound of the voice that did the speaking, which some attributed to an angel. In fairness, it's likely they didn't realize it was the voice of God. Thunder and a voice are radically different sounds, just like different languages are different and those present could all hear something different on that day.

> The miracle that happened at Pentecost was not necessarily that one was happening in what was being **spoken**, but a miracle in what was being **heard** by those from the other regions down below the upper room.

It doesn't matter whether or not the original people in the upper room spoke in native tongues; the people would not have been able to hear it without a miraculous intervention from God enabling them to hear it.

Note

1. I will go into more detail about how to lead someone in the baptism in the Holy Spirit in the appendix of this book.

Chapter 11

Speaking in Tongues Is Just One Evidence of the Baptism

*S*ections in this chapter were cowritten by Brian Parkman. I saw him once get asked these questions on his Facebook wall a few years ago and I thought he gave a stellar response that I had never thought of before. With his permission I modified it to include his words in a blog posting on *Fire Press*, of which I've since removed and reworked and edited to include here as a chapter of its own, along with some of my own additional commentary. As a result, it would be highly inappropriate to not give him credit for basically cowriting this chapter with me.

The True Evidence? *(Brian Parkman)*

Brian was asked the following question: "Do you believe that speaking in tongues is the only true evidence of the baptism in the Holy Spirit?" Here is his response.

> **The ultimate purpose of receiving the Holy Spirit is power, but the initial evidence is tongues.**

No, but it's the only *verifiable initial* evidence that one has been baptized in the Holy Spirit. Let me explain: the baptism in the Holy Spirit is unique to the New Testament believer. Therefore we have to have an *initial* evidence that is also unique to the New Testament in order to know one has been filled the moment we are praying for them. Otherwise, how would I know they have been filled at that moment? When Peter and his brethren went to Cornelius's house in Acts 10, and the Holy Spirit fell on them, how did they know that the Holy Spirit had fallen on them?

"For they heard them speak with other tongues" (Acts 10:46). That was the only *initial* evidence they had. Otherwise how would they have known? The ultimate purpose of receiving the Holy Spirit is power, but the initial evidence is tongues, otherwise there is no way for me to definitively know they have been filled when I pray for them.

You might ask, "What if you laid hands on them to be filled, and all they did was prophesy?" That still would not be conclusive evidence they had been baptized in the Holy Spirit because they prophesied in the Old Testament too. The Holy Spirit may just be coming on them at that moment and they prophesy, but that doesn't necessarily mean they have been filled with the Holy Spirit, because they prophesied in the Old Testament without being baptized in the Holy Spirit.

An experience unique to the New Testament needs evidence that is also unique to the New Testament in order to know they have received the New Testament experience of Spirit baptism. Any other evidence you can name to "prove" they are baptized in the Holy Spirit happened in the Old Testament as well. Tongues didn't happen in the Old Covenant, but is exclusive to the New Covenant, so it is the only conclusive initial evidence we have to know they have been baptized in the Holy Spirit at that moment.

Examples of the Gifts in the Old Testament *(Steve Bremner)*

The gift of a word of wisdom reveals a fraction of the mind of God concerning people, places, or things pertaining to the future. Moses told Israel as they left Egypt and entered the Promised Land what would happen if they disobeyed the voice of God; likewise, Samuel told Israel all that would happen if they appointed a king over them.

A word of knowledge by contrast is a revelation by the Holy Spirit giving a piece of God's knowledge or information concerning people and situations in the present. Joshua received a word of knowledge about why the city of Ai was not taken (Joshua 7:10-13). Elisha knew by miraculous revelation the location of the Syrian camp, thereby saving Israel from being attacked (2 Kings 6:8-23).

The discerning of spirits is the supernatural ability to see into the spirit world—by this insight the believer can see angels, demons, and discern the condition of the human spirit, whether good or bad. An example of this would be when Elisha prayed for the eyes of his servant to be opened and he then saw the angel armies of the Lord who were surrounding them (2 Kings 6:17).

> **An experience unique to the New Testament needs evidence that is also unique to the New Testament in order to know they have received the New Testament experience of Spirit baptism.**

The gift of faith is a supernatural manifestation by the Holy Spirit supplying *unlimited faith* in a specific situation to achieve supernatural results, as evidenced in the example of Daniel in the lion's den (Daniel 6:23).

For our purposes, we're defining the gifts of healings as the supernatural impartation of God's divine healing power through us to cure disease and heal the sick and afflicted instantly—in particular, being anointed to minister healing for specific kinds of sicknesses. This happened *many* times throughout the Old Testament and we assume the reader can think of a few examples for him- or herself.

What distinguishes the working of miracles from the gifts of healing, however, is that it's a special momentary gift of authority which enables us, by the anointing of God, to intervene in the ordinary course of nature to do something that could not be done naturally. A true miracle must involve the suspension of natural laws in the ordinary course of nature. Examples include the multiplying of the widow's oil (2 Kings 4:1-7), parting the Red Sea and walking on dry ground (Exodus 14:13-31), and the floating axe head (2 Kings 6:1-7), among many others.

Why the Evidence of Spirit Baptism Is Not Prophesying or Having the Gift of Prophecy *(Steve Bremner)*

The gift of prophecy is a supernatural utterance in a known tongue—not conceived by human thought or reasoning—spoken under the anointing of God to exhort, edify, encourage, strengthen, and comfort the church. F. F. Bruce says that prophecy is to "declare the mind of God in the power of the Spirit," while a prophet is "a divinely called and inspired speaker who receives authoritative revelations directly from the heart of God and is compelled to deliver them publicly."

To continue the line of Brian's thought that one can point to Old Testament Scriptures to show that people operated in all of the gifts of the Spirit mentioned in the New Testament, except for tongues, I point to King Saul. In 1 Samuel 10, when the prophet Samuel anointed him king of Israel, it states that the Spirit of the Lord rushed upon him and he prophesied with the prophets (1 Samuel 10:6, 9-13). Then, later on, once he had backslidden and was trying to kill the young David whom God had appointed to replace Saul, it says, "Now the Spirit of the Lord departed from Saul, and a harmful spirit from the Lord tormented him" (1 Samuel 16:14).

The Spirit of God had left Saul at this point, and Saul no longer walked in any kind of anointing, but was troubled instead by a tormenting spirit (from God at that!). Later on, during which time Saul was trying to kill David—not very good fruit for someone if they have the Holy Spirit—it states in 1 Samuel 19:23-24:

> *And [Saul] went there to Naioth in Ramah. And the Spirit of God came upon him also, and as he went he*

*prophesied until he came to Naioth in Ramah. And he **too stripped off his clothes, and he too prophesied** before Samuel and lay naked all that day and all that night. Thus it is said, "Is Saul also among the prophets?"*

So let's get this straight: in the Old Testament, before Christ's work on the cross and before believers were able to get saved and have the Holy Spirit living inside of them, we had instances of murderous backslidden kings prophesying naked when the Spirit came upon them? Therefore, I would not necessarily point to prophesying as evidence of being filled with the Spirit. If anything, this example can be used for encouragement for the New Testament believer that prophesying is *easier* than we think, and all can do it. I'd encourage the reader to give a thorough reading of 1 Corinthians 14 for more about the gifts in a local fellowship context.

Gifts and Fruit without Baptism? *(Brian Parkman)*

The next question Brian was asked was, "Can we show the fruit of the Spirit and the gifts of the Spirit without being baptized in the Holy Spirit?" He responds below.

> **Faith still works without being baptized in the Holy Spirit.**

Yes, one can show the fruit of the Spirit without being baptized in the Holy Spirit. It's not the fruit of the baptism in the

Holy Spirit, it's the fruit of being *born* of the Spirit, or being born again. There are plenty of Christians who walk in the fruit of the Spirit and aren't baptized in the Holy Spirit.

Now whether one walks in the gifts of the Spirit without being baptized in the Holy Spirit—generally speaking, they don't. But take healing for instance. A person could still get someone healed and not be baptized in the Holy Spirit because they can still pray for them *by faith,* and the person can receive their healing through faith. But strictly speaking, that wouldn't necessarily be a gift of the Spirit but it was the person's faith that healed them. Smith Wigglesworth got people healed before he was baptized in the Spirit just because he still believed in divine healing and had faith for it. Faith still works without being baptized in the Holy Spirit.

Since speaking in tongues is the only evidence of being baptized in the Holy Spirit that is *exclusive* to the New Testament, tongues is the only definitive evidence I have that someone is baptized in the Holy Spirit. A person could be getting people healed, but that doesn't definitively show me they are baptized in the Holy Spirit because they healed in the Old Testament too, and they weren't baptized in the Holy Spirit under that covenant. That person may just have a strong faith for healing, or he or she may be ministering the Word on healing so well to those he prays for are getting healed by their own faith. It could also just be a temporary endowment of power like in the Old Testament—like the way the Spirit rushed on King Saul, who was deemed wicked by that point in his life.

So tongues being the only gift of the Spirit that did not appear in the Old Testament, it becomes the only gifting that we can definitively "see" in a person's life that lets us know they are baptized in the Holy Spirit in the New Testament sense. The other giftings wouldn't be conclusive because the Old Testament shows us one can do those other things without being baptized in the Holy Spirit. Theoretically one could operate in the gifts without being baptized in the Holy Ghost, because it could just be a temporary endowment by the Holy Spirit for that moment, but generally speaking most of the people you see operating in the gifts are baptized in the Holy Spirit.

To summarize, I would not suggest that speaking in tongues is just one of many evidences of Spirit baptism, because we can see operations of all of the other gifts of the Spirt in some form in the Old Testament before a new covenant was enacted with the Holy Spirit coming to dwell in us. In order to have evidence of a new covenant, there needs to be some kind of sign exclusive to the new covenant, which we believe is the gift or sign of speaking in tongues.

Chapter 12

One Can't Speak in Tongues at Will

As a missionary, I oftentimes come across individuals in Peru who have the ability to speak in tongues but they don't take any initiative of their own to do so. They're waiting for what I call a "validating experience." For example, maybe when they were first baptized with the Holy Spirit they had some kind of spectacular experience along with it. Maybe they fell to the floor or they had strong ecstatic sensations or uncontrollable bouts of laughter or some other such experiences. Because they were also able to speak in tongues on that occasion, I've noticed that, generally speaking, these same individuals often assume they need to have ecstatic experiences again or their speaking in tongues is not "legit."

I've heard students of mine in our ministry school make mention of how they "knew" it was appropriate to release a tongue or flow in their prayer language because of an anointing they could tangibly sense in their body or emotions, and which gave them confidence to pray in the Spirit. Now, when it comes to the corporate gift in an assembly with other believers present where an interpretation is required, yes, this would be appropriate. I would encourage others to obey the Lord's leading in such times, but not when it comes to building up your own inner man through praying in tongues, the personal prayer language. You can yield to the latter at will. You can instigate this and take the initiative. A great man of God, Smith Wigglesworth, is attributed with a quote along the lines of, "I don't wait for the Spirit to move me; I move the Spirit!" To those who think we need a validating experience or that God "only does things in his proper sovereignty," that quote can sound rather arrogant and blasphemous, but I assure you that it's not.

> **When we look at the text in various translations it invariably says *they* (the individuals) did the speaking *as* the Spirit gave them utterance, or as the Spirit "led them."**

This is one of the biggest misconceptions charismatics and Pentecostals have. Whenever I lead people in a prayer to receive the baptism in the Holy Spirit, I encourage them to expect to speak in tongues by showing them the text in Acts 2. I then ask an individual to read out loud verses 3 and 4 and ask him or her *who* did the speaking. Three quarters of the time the first answer is "the Holy Spirit." But when we look at the text in various translations it invariably says *they* (the individuals) did the speaking *as* the Spirit gave them utterance, or as the Spirit "led them." If you are reading this and have never spoken in tongues before due to having misconceptions like this, allow me to tear down this barrier for you.

> **You are able to control yourself. You can ignore the leading to call the person or speak and declare a prophetic word to someone.**

Have you ever "felt led" by the Holy Spirit to share a word with someone? Maybe you are praying for a friend to give his life to Jesus, and the Holy Spirit places it on your heart to call the person on the phone, and so in obedience to that gentle nudging you reach for your phone and call that particular individual. Wouldn't you know, it just so happened to be a great thing that you called them because right at that moment they needed to be encouraged. The Holy Spirit didn't call the person, you did.

Jack Hayford says this about the gift of tongues:

> The miracle of speaking in tongues is a case of cooperation between humanity and deity. We speak in spiritual languages because we choose to allow the Holy Spirit to express Himself through us in that way. The Holy Spirit is the source—we cooperate. This does not mean that we lose control of our abilities and the Holy Spirit takes over. God never works like that. He gives us the gift and we have to choose to exercise it. God doesn't do anything without our involvement and partnership with Him. On the contrary, every time we speak with tongues we are exercising our faith and are cooperating with the Holy Spirit.[1]

I like to compare the "leading" to speak in tongues with any other leading you get from the Holy Spirit. You are able to control yourself. You are able to decide whether or not to do it. You can ignore the leading to call the person or speak and declare a prophetic word to someone. The tongues come from the same place in your inner man where the Spirit of God is communicating to you on the inside. You are merely choosing to put your own voice to these weird-sounding syllables, and release them out of your own mouth.

About this, the apostle Paul said, "If I pray in a tongue, my spirit prays but my mind is unfruitful. What am I to do? I will pray with my spirit, but I will pray with my mind also; I will sing praise with my spirit, but I will sing with my mind also" (1 Corinthians 14:14-15).

Notice that he uses a verb that denotes how he uses his own volition, or his own willpower, when doing this praying: "I *will* pray with my mind, and I *will* also pray with my understanding." Personal experience and my understanding of these words of Scripture indicate to me that the believer has full control of his or her faculties, leading to the conclusion that speaking in tongues is quite simple and actually not complicated at all. Therefore Paul referred to this as praying without understanding or he wouldn't have made the comparison to occasions when he prayed and sung with his understanding.

> **Paul was not forbidding speaking in tongues
> or insisting on any kind of conditions
> for one's personal prayer language.**

Edification Is Not a Feeling

Personally, 95 percent of the time I don't feel anything when praying in tongues. In the moment when I'm praying, I might not have understanding as to what I'm praying about, but the understanding can come later in the form of revelation or insight into the Scriptures or sensitivity to the Spirit. This is why Paul mentioned in verse 13 that we should pray for an interpretation of the tongues we speak. Why? So we can be a benefit to others:

> *Otherwise, if you give thanks with your spirit, how can anyone in the position of an outsider say "Amen" to your thanksgiving when he does not know what you are saying? For you may be giving thanks well enough, but the other person is not being built up. I thank God that I speak in tongues more than all of you. Nevertheless, in church I would rather speak five words with my mind in order to instruct others, than ten thousand words in a tongue.* (1 Corinthians 14:16-18)

So yes, in a corporate gathering, it would be much more beneficial for others if you were speaking in a language that everyone present understood. However, Paul was not forbidding speaking in tongues or insisting on any kind of conditions for one's personal prayer language.

Here in Peru, whenever we gather together, we oftentimes have three languages represented: the first and most common being Spanish, since that's the native language here; second to that is the English that the missionaries such as myself speak; and the third language is Shipibo, which is the native tongue some of our fellowship speak in the jungle where they come from. Since Spanish is the language we all have in common, our time together of worship, singing, fellowshipping, and praying is all typically done in Spanish. It's simply more practical for us to operate in a language where everybody benefits and can understand what is going on.

In one sense, it's true that you can't pray in tongues if not for the Holy Spirit's involvement any more than you can't accept Jesus if not for the sacrifice he paid on the cross, but that's not to say you need to feel a special glory ball or some kind of ecstatic tingling sensation.

Recall the story of Samson in the Old Testament book of Judges.

> *When Delilah saw that [Samson] had told her all his heart, she sent and called the lords of the Philistines, saying, "Come up again, for he has told me all his heart." Then the lords of the Philistines came up to her and brought the money in their hands. She made him sleep on her knees. And she called a man and had him shave off the seven locks of his head. Then she began to torment him, and his strength left him. And she said, "The Philistines are upon you, Samson!" And he awoke from his sleep and said, "I will go out as at other times and shake myself free."* **But he did not know that the Lord had left him**. (Judges 16:18-20)

If you read through the chapters about Samson's life in the book of Judges it should strike you that he didn't know the Lord had left him. What is so significant about that? One thing at the very least: if Samson couldn't tell the presence of the Lord, or "the anointing," was missing, then he probably couldn't tell when it was present either. It probably didn't have a special "anointy" feeling. He thought to himself that he'd just do what he had always done and shake himself free from the cords that bound him but couldn't notice a difference.

Other verses in the book of Judges describe instances where the Spirit of the Lord came on Samson in some kind of force to get something accomplished that he couldn't have done in his own strength, such as described in Judges 14:6, 14:19, and 15:14. We know that the power in his strength did not lie in the fact that no razor had touched his head, but in the obedience of doing what he was instructed to do by the Lord, which was to not cut his hair or shave his head, and drink no strong drink because he was consecrated to the Lord.

Think about this for a moment. Most Christians tend to know this story and that he had a lust problem. He was sleeping with a prostitute, and despite the multiple marriages—or marriage attempts anyway—God still used him in a mighty way to single-handedly kill thousands of Philistines. My point in drawing your attention to Judges 16 is not to say that you can keep engaging in sexual immorality or lying and still be anointed. Every time Delilah asked him the secret to his strength, he lied to her and the power of God was still on him to break free from the ropes each time the Philistines came upon him.

This passage probably messes with popular charismatic theology. Does it bother you that God still used Samson in power despite his obvious sin? I submit to you for consideration that the anointing of God is more mechanical than it is relational. I hope you're not reading this to say that I'm advocating that we can live in sin and still operate in the anointing. You don't need to live a holy life to be used by God because you and I are expendable to the Lord's purposes. He can, does, and will work despite us, not because he needs us. The writer of Hebrews reminds us that without holiness we will not see the Lord (Hebrews 12:14).

> Let's not be like Samson who didn't know when the Lord left him, or furthermore let us not be like any to whom Jesus will say, "Yes, you did do these things for me, but I don't know you."

Samson was a man consumed with lust and a bad temper, and he still did great exploits for the Lord. But he didn't know the presence of the Lord had left him. Can I submit to you for consideration that this implies he didn't know the difference between when the anointing power of the Lord was upon him or when it wasn't? It probably didn't feel like anything special.

I don't want to be like Samson, being able to do great exploits for the Lord when my lifestyle and heart are not right with him. It is significant that in Matthew 7:21-23, when individuals tell Jesus on judgment day about all the exploits they did in his name, they were all miraculous: prophesying, casting out demons, and healing the sick. These are not activities unsaved people are doing in the bars and clubs. At least not that I've ever discovered.

Jesus will tell them he didn't know them even though they were actually doing miraculous deeds in his name, and yet they'll still be cast out of his presence in the end. Sobering stuff to think about indeed. Let's not be like Samson who didn't know when the Lord left him, or furthermore let us not be like any to whom

Jesus will say, "Yes, you did do these things for me, but I don't know you."

> **The edification process that comes with prolonged amounts of speaking and praying in tongues results in change, not in sensations or feelings.**

"Steve, what on earth does all this talk about the presence of God and the anointing have to do with speaking in tongues exactly?" you may be thinking here. If feeling something has nothing to do with whether or not the presence of God is available or "on you," then likewise it means you don't need to wait until you feel something special in order to operate in the power of God, which includes speaking in tongues. I repeat, you don't need to feel anything to speak in tongues.

Some charismatic preachers mistakenly believe that if they pray in tongues diligently every day for a certain amount of time—let's arbitrarily say three months—then when they get on stage suddenly one day their preaching will just be amazing and everybody they lay hands on will fall to the floor and shake, bake, rattle and roll, and they'll have an uproariously glorious church service. However, what's more likely to happen is that maybe, after the end of three months, you will find that you can't approach God in prayer without the feeling that you need to stop exaggerating when you preach. Maybe a stronger conviction will come on you and you no longer can keep watching that cable TV show you used to be such a fan of because something bothers you about it. You might feel led to delete things from the hard drive of your computer or throw away DVDs you own. The edification process that comes with prolonged amounts of speaking and praying in tongues results in change, not in sensations or feelings. If you get sensations of the glory of God or other feelings, then that's just gravy on top of what God is doing in your heart.

In conclusion, the speaker always has control of himself or herself when it comes to this particular diversity of tongues (personal edification). He or she can start and stop their tongues as they wish. Out of respect for the anointing of the Holy Spirit, many have overcomplicated this particular gift out of fear of abusing it or "playing with strange fire." Go for it. Pray in tongues a lot, and pray in tongues often! You won't regret the long-term results.

Note

1. Jack Hayford, *Grounds for Living* (Tonbridge, England, Sovereign World Ltd.), 172.

Chapter 13

Other Objections

*I*n this chapter I want to list other objections that can be answered much more simply and don't require the time and space to cover in an entire chapter. The first three are also heavily gleaned from Steve Thompson's book *You May All Prophesy,* but I've taken the liberty to reword them enough that they are no longer directly quoting from his chapter on myths and fallacies of the prophetic.

We Really Need the Fruit of the Spirit, Not the Gifts

One of the major objections when it comes to being baptized in the Holy Spirit is this: "We don't need the gifts of the Spirit; what we really need is the fruit of the Spirit!"

This may sound balanced, but it's biblically inaccurate. While seeking spiritual gifts without cultivating spiritual fruit is an error, we should never attempt to correct it by devaluing the importance of spiritual gifts in the life of the body of Christ. This teaching also exposes a subtle form of pride that implies we do not need spiritual gifts at all. When we understand that spiritual gifts are *empowerments* provided by God to manifest his kingdom, our attitude toward them will change. They will no longer be seen as optional. Words of knowledge, words of wisdom, and discerning of spirits are tools in the same way that guns, ammunition, and grenades are tools for a soldier.

At the beginning of his letter to the Corinthians, Paul makes a statement that shows he understood the importance of spiritual gifts in his ministry—he said his testimony was proven to the Corinthians by the fact *they* were functioning in the spiritual gifts (1 Corinthians 1:4-7). Paul goes on to say in his letter that his testimony concerning Christ was with power and demonstration and not just words of human wisdom (1 Corinthians 2:1-5). It has been suggested that Acts 17:22–18:1 shows that Paul had limited results when he preached in Athens using *only* his intellect and ability to reason.

> **This teaching also exposes a subtle form of pride that implies we do not need spiritual gifts at all.**

Also, nowhere in the New Testament are we told to choose between the gifts of the Spirit or the fruit of the Spirit. James C. Davidson says concerning this:

> The Bible says we should have both gifts and fruit! If a Christian experiencing the gifts is not showing the fruit, that isn't an argument against the gifts. But it

does show that God the Holy Spirit can take ordinary and unsatisfactory material and work through them to God's glory.[1]

The Holy Spirit's work within the believer produces the following fruit: love, joy, peace, patience, kindness, goodness, faithfulness, gentleness, and self-control (Galatians 5:22-23). Jesus told his disciples the Holy Spirit would be *with* them and *in* them (John 14:17), but then he also told them to not leave Jerusalem until they received power from on high. This obviously is a different experience altogether than when they received the Holy Spirit within, or else Jesus would have been mistaken or foolish to tell them not to leave Jerusalem until they received something they already had.

It's interesting to note also that we have two groups of nine connected with the work of the Holy Spirit—nine fruit in Galatians 5 and nine gifts in 1 Corinthians 12:7-11. The fruit might be referred to as the *character traits* resulting from the indwelling of the Holy Spirit: fruit grows on the branch because of the life within the tree. The fruit of the Spirit is demonstrative of the indwelling and fruit bearing of the Holy Spirit in our lives as individual believers. The gifts of the Spirit are for service to the body of Christ and the lost, and not us, as a community where each individual constituting the whole does its part.

Seek the Giver, Not His Gifts

Another objection to the baptism in in the Holy Spirit is, "We should seek the giver of spiritual gifts, not the gifts themselves."

While this makes for a great sermon, it is also biblically inaccurate. In a sense, if we reject the gifts God has for us, which include but are not limited to the personal prayer language of speaking in tongues, we are in some ways rejecting him, since he has given spiritual gifts as a manifestation *of* himself in our midst. Likewise, praying in tongues is a way to receive revelation and speak mysteries, which in turn enhance our intimacy with our heavenly Father, the giver of such a gift.

We must understand that the Corinthians were already functioning in the gifts when Paul made this statement to them at the beginning of his letter (1 Corinthians 1:7), but they were *abusing* the gifts, speaking out of order, and so on. To bring a balanced correction, Paul, a mature man of God—and apostle, of course— offered instruction about the gifts and wisdom for their use. But he never instructed them *not* to seek the gifts, nor did he criticize them for being too focused on spiritual gifts. Rather, the exact opposite occurred: he urged them to earnestly covet them.

> **If we reject the gifts God has for us, which include but are not limited to the personal prayer language of speaking in tongues, we are in some ways rejecting him, since he has given spiritual gifts as a manifestation *of* himself in our midst.**

The same Greek word translated "earnestly covet" can be translated as "zealously lust." Immediately following this in the "love chapter," Paul proceeds to launch into a profound discourse on the proper motivation and manner in which the gifts are to be used, which is love. When reading this book of the Bible, the point is not to overemphasize chapters 12 and 14 at the exclusion of chapter 13, nor is it to read chapter 13 but shut one's brain off when reading chapters 12 and 14, which give clear teaching on tongues, congregational tongues with interpretation, and prophesying corporately in particular. Love and the gifts are a part of the same package. Paul was imploring them to operate in the *gifts* out of a heart of *love* for one another.

Seeking Spiritual Gifts Is Selfish

When someone says that seeking spiritual gifts is selfish, it is similar to the "seeking the giver not the gifts" misconception. While it's true that some will have questionable motives, God will ultimately deal with character issues as he sees fit. However, this concept is still biblically inaccurate since the spiritual gifts are given in order to minister to *others*. Serving others is not selfish. Just because it's possible to desire to minister with a heart full of mixed motives doesn't mean we are to *not bother* seeking ways to minister to others. Have you ever been used of God even though you have or had sinful issues to deal with?

Think of Paul's response in Philippians 1:15-18 when talking of people ministering with questionable motives. He didn't react to the fact that people were preaching the gospel out of selfish ambition. Rather, he *rejoiced* that the gospel was being preached. Again, Paul never discouraged anyone from seeking the gifts, and neither should we. Let God deal with people and their bad motives as he sees fit.

We Should Speak Words
People Can Understand

Some people say, "Well, Paul said he'd rather speak five words in an understood language than many words in tongues. That sounds to me like we shouldn't bother with tongues at all."

167

Tongues are a great means for giving God thanks. In 1 Corinthians 14:15-17 Paul was correcting the Corinthian believers in their overuse of giving thanks using this divine language *publicly*, since an unlearned person in spiritual things would not be able to understand what Paul was saying if he were to proceed to give thanks in tongues in their presence. But notice, however, that he indicates that tongues are a great way of praising God when he says "you give thanks well" (1 Corinthians 14:17). People have objected to the use of the personal prayer language in public meetings, since Paul states emphatically in the epistle to the Corinthians that he'd rather speak five words with his understanding so that he could teach others, than ten thousand words in a tongue (1 Corinthians 14:19).

Paul says that the believers should seek gifts of the Spirit that would cause edification of the whole body, not just edification of themselves (1 Corinthians 14:12). Notice that Paul *only* objects to giving thanks publicly in tongues for the sake of an uninformed person in spiritual matters who would not understand or be able to relate to what was taking place in the meeting. What if a group of believers were together and none among them were uninformed and all were filled with the Holy Spirit and exercised the gift of tongues? Surely this set of rules would not apply to that setting; rather, they would be free to worship and praise in tongues.

You Don't Need to Speak in Tongues to Be Baptized in the Holy Spirit

Someone may object, "You don't need to speak in tongues to be baptized in the Holy Spirit." This one is tricky, and it may just boil down to a matter of semantics for some readers. Another way of saying it is that someone can be baptized or filled with the Holy Spirit without speaking in tongues.

Before addressing this thought, however, allow me to say you don't need to do *anything* to be baptized in the Holy Spirit. You don't have to speak in tongues, but you do *get* to. We're granted this privilege as a gift, but it's not an obligation by any means. People can neglect to pray in tongues and miss out on the benefits of doing so if they truly wish. With all the understanding I've laid out in the hopes of removing these obstacles in the previous chapters, in the next section we'll focus more on the benefits of doing so.

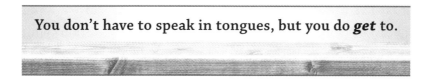

You don't have to speak in tongues, but you do *get* to.

In Acts 19 Paul met disciples of John the Baptist. Paul asked them if they received the Holy Spirit since they believed. Obviously these disciples would be believers in God and go to heaven if they died without having spoken in tongues. This is not disputed. But notice here that Paul evidently thought they could be believers and still not be walking in the dimensions of the Holy Spirit he was familiar with, and sought to find out about their state.

Paul did not ask them if God had *given* them the Holy Spirit since they believed, but if they had *received* the Holy Spirit since they believed in the gospel of repentance. There's a substantial difference between giving and receiving. Just as God has given or offers salvation through his Son Jesus Christ doesn't mean everybody has or will choose to receive the salvation gift. The same is true with everything else God offers as a gift. He has sent the Holy Spirit to the earth to indwell the believer, but now there is the gift of speaking in tongues that can be accessed and used in personal edification. Paul does not seem to have told them here that they were not saved if they didn't receive the Holy Spirit. He merely asked, and they said that they didn't even know there was a Holy Spirit.

Let's take this apart for a few moments. To repeat what I've already stated, you are saved if you don't speak in tongues. In fact, you will go to heaven if you don't speak in tongues. Only an overzealous charismatic with incredibly limited understanding of speaking in tongues and salvation will tell you otherwise. But, as I've presented in an earlier chapter, this clearly is a post-conversion work that would ideally be part of salvation, which we would not have to worry about if all believers were filled or baptized in the Spirit.

Does speaking in tongues accompany the baptism in the Holy Spirit? Yes, typically it does. And if we use our Scriptures as the basis to form this opinion, I don't believe we'd be having this debate.

Prayed Many Times with No Results

Another common objection to receiving the baptism in the Holy Spirit is, "I've been prayed for many times to receive the baptism in the Holy Spirit and I still don't speak in tongues; therefore, it is not evidence of being filled with the Spirit."

I can't possibly know why experiencing this gift may be difficult for you personally, and if we were to have a face-to-face conversation I might be able to locate what the mental barrier may be. There are many misconceptions and misunderstandings people have as to what happens, such as believing the Holy Spirit will come and shake their tongue around and make words come out of their mouth without them trying. I often ask people if they've ever prophesied or shared things that they were inspired of the Holy Spirit. If you have ever done this, then speaking in tongues is just as easy, and it is simply speaking the inspired utterances that come from within but don't make any sense to you.

Usually, when people tell me they've been prayed for many times, they've not had the validating experience, or they have had false expectations regarding what will happen. I encourage you to read "How to Lead Someone in the Baptism in the Holy Spirit" in the appendix of this book. You'll be able to glean from that if you are a "receiver."

> **In the Bible they didn't seem to be getting filled with demons when they spoke in tongues.**

Tongues Are of the Devil

The whole "tongues being of the devil" thing always got me confused too, because in the Bible they didn't seem to be getting filled with demons when they spoke in tongues. Even though it doesn't specifically mention tongues, Luke 11:11-13 makes it pretty clear that God will not trick us, giving us something else entirely when asking for his Spirit:

> *What father among you, if his son asks for a fish, will instead of a fish give him a serpent; or if he asks*

for an egg, will give him a scorpion? If you then, who are evil, know how to give good gifts to your children, how much more will the heavenly Father give the Holy Spirit to those who ask him!

Can you imagine some filthy heathen rebels standing on a street corner outside of a Pentecostal church while all the congregants exited the building after a Sunday morning service and they overhear some of the congregants speaking in tongues. And as they walk out one of the heathen says to the other, "What is that thing they're saying?" The other responds, "Oh, haven't you heard? Why, they're speaking in tongues—but it's of the devil, you know!" Then the other unsaved guy scratches his head, and says to him, "Well, if it were of the devil, wouldn't we be doing it too?" It's quite silly when you think about it!

Speaking Too Much in Tongues

This last objection is that a person can speak too much in tongues. My only answer to that is simple: how can you possibly edify yourself too much?

Note

1. James C. Davidson, *This Happy Gift of Tongues,* Location 248, Kindle.

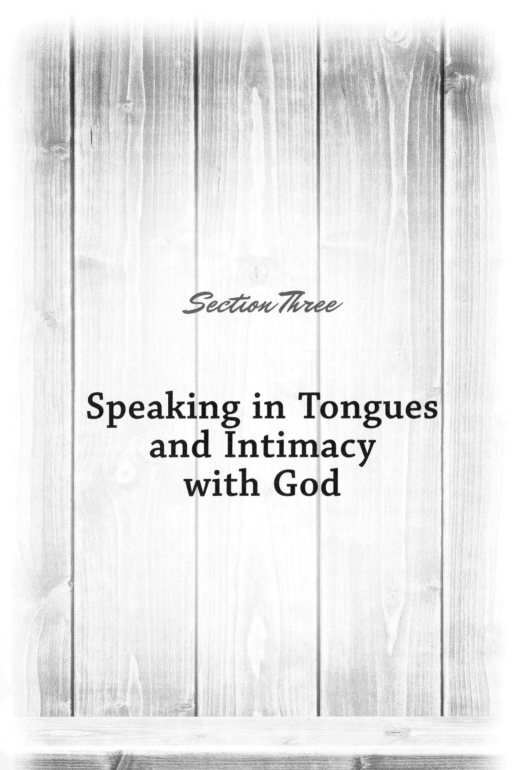

Section Three

Speaking in Tongues
and Intimacy
with God

Chapter 14

Reasons Why Every Believer Should Speak in Tongues

As we've stated and repeated several times in this book, when you speak or pray in a tongue you edify yourself (1 Corinthians 14:4). Paul encouraged the believers at Corinth to continue the practice of speaking with other tongues in their worship of God and in their private prayer lives as a means of spiritual edification. When praying in the Spirit, you are in effect praying directly to God in a manner that people who may overhear your words would not understand what you are saying, but the Holy Spirit is directly involved in your prayers all the same.

> **Your spirit is where all permanent change comes from, not by your mind or willpower alone.**

First Corinthians 3:16 and 6:19 both refer to the believer as the temple of the Holy Spirit. It is this temple that the Holy Spirit is building for himself to abide in whenever we pray in the Spirit (pray in tongues) since "edify" simply means "to build." The believer may not even feel emotionally or physically as though the prayer is being answered, but that's mostly because this is spiritual edification taking place, not emotional or physical edification.

Dave Roberson teaches in his book *The Walk of the Spirit, The Walk of Power* that your spirit is the one getting the answer to your prayers because it's your spirit doing the praying (1 Corinthians 14:14). Furthermore, your spirit is where all permanent change comes from, not by your mind or willpower alone.[1] Out of necessity, if we're praying in the Spirit and preparing a place for the Holy Ghost to rule our lives by doing so, then the things that don't belong in God's plan, like our flesh and sinful nature, will be purged from us.

Speaking in tongues helps serve as a reminder of the Holy Spirit's indwelling presence in our hearts (John 14:16-17). These tongues are a flowing stream that should never dry up, continually enriching life for years to come. If we can be conscious of the indwelling presence of the Spirit of God every day, then it is bound to affect the way we live since it is the Holy Spirit who changes us from the inside out, not our own willpower or decision making.

Another reason to consider praying in tongues is that the believer is praying in line with God's perfect will. Just because the believer knows *how* to pray doesn't mean we know *for what* to pray as we ought, and therefore also, since it is the Spirit of God inspiring our praying, it helps eliminate selfishness from our prayers. Romans 8:27-28 talks about how the Holy Spirit continually searches our hearts. Dave Roberson teaches that the Holy Spirit does this with the intention of removing everything that is contrary to the will of God. Then the Holy Spirit replaces it with the plan he heard for our personal life when God formulated his plan for us. We are too ignorant to pray about our lives and things like our call, so the Holy Spirit's great reservoir of wisdom and counsel resides within our spirits just waiting to be released with tongues.[2]

A simple analogy is worth mentioning here to get this point across. As ambassadors of Christ on the earth (2 Corinthians 5:20), the believer is here to represent another kingdom, one he or she currently doesn't geographically reside in—the kingdom of heaven. An ambassador represents the person or nation they're sent by. For example, an embassy for the United States located in another country doesn't get its authority from the country it is in, but from the country it's representing. Despite the fact that this embassy is *geographically* located on foreign soil, it is not under the *influence* of the government of that country. An embassy worker's salary is paid by the country that worker is representing and is in no way based on the economic climate of foreign country in which they reside. They are *in* that country but not *of* that country, much like the believer is in this world but not of the world. Christians are here on this earth representing the one who sent them, Jesus Christ.

To relate this all to tongues, consider how the ambassador communicates with his or her homeland. They typically have a mode of communication or a channel that the citizens of that country don't know about and are not able to access. The ambassador can receive orders from their homeland, which could be through encrypted Internet communication or secret phone lines. As Christians, we are representatives of the King in heaven and can receive orders from a mode of communication that affects our spirit, enabling us to receive orders while not necessarily knowing in our mind what they are.

This way our enemy, satan, can't get us to accidentally reveal any secrets under the threat of torture or death, since we are dead to ourselves in Christ (Romans 6:2-3, 6-7). We don't know any of the secrets we've been praying about in the Spirit. The Holy Spirit hears what is being spoken out at God's throne and can bring that message and inspire us to pray in a language that we don't understand with our mental faculties. Yet in doing this we are still praying out the will of God—all the while bypassing our mind.

It's a brilliant idea of God's, eh? Why would a believer not want to practice this? Since this gift is so effective in building us up, it's no surprise the enemy has done such a wonderful job not only convincing people it's not necessary but that actually doing so is evil or strange.

> Praying in tongues does nothing but enhance the working of the Word on the inside of us, causing us to receive and walk in more of God's power as we become more yielded to him.

The Holy Spirit Is Our Teacher

As mentioned earlier, the Holy Spirit can bypass our minds and put God's will into our hearts without us even necessarily knowing it. As well as edifying us personally, speaking in tongues can help inoculate us against false teaching. First John 5:7 says the Spirit and the Word are one, therefore if the Spirit is in you inspiring your prayers, you are not going to be praying prayers that contradict the Word of God. Rather, an increased hunger should take place in you since you are now praying according to the will of the one who wrote the Word.

Praying in tongues never takes away from the Word of God; instead, it builds up our spirit by giving us greater understanding of the revelation knowledge already contained in the Word. This kind of praying does nothing but enhance the working of the Word on the inside of us, causing us to receive and walk in more of God's power as we become more yielded to him. As the Holy Spirit is praying God's will through us, he is in total agreement with the written Word.

This is also why the devil has removed tongues from three quarters of the church—it's much easier for believers to be deceived by the ever-changing doctrines of humans when they have been separated from one of the primary teaching tools that enables them to learn from the Holy Spirit himself![3] Dave Roberson writes, "If there were only one door that the devil could keep you from entering, it would be the door of praying in tongues. He hates it second only to salvation and wants to make sure you never go through it."[4]

The first two years of my Christian life I never heard anything on the baptism in the Holy Spirit, and hence never learned about praying in tongues until I started attending a charismatic church in my hometown with a friend I met one summer. At first, the difference in lifestyle among these believers was shocking to me as they had a passion for worship and personal holiness

I was not seeing among my non-charismatic friends. The more teaching I received about the spiritual gifts and their functions, the more I started to see how the cessationist viewpoint that I'd grown up with was not founded on anything biblical. Again, I don't say this to judge or imply that non-charismatics don't seek after holiness; I'm only stating that I wasn't experiencing or seeing much of it in my personal context.

> The devil knows what a threat a believer, who can tap into this revelation knowledge and edification process through a personal tutor like the Holy Spirit, is to the kingdom of darkness.

My life radically changed after I got baptized in the Holy Spirit and, more specifically, as I prayed in tongues almost a minimum of an hour a day. I experienced a lot of death to myself and many habits in my life during this time, including specific sins I was bound by just seemed to fall off of me. I was truly a completely different person from the inside out as a result of praying in this manner on a regular basis. The sinful habits that kept me bound were suddenly no longer a problem and I felt like I was walking in new dimensions of Christianity I had never experienced even in my most amazing mountaintop experiences. Not only that, but my Bible reading and study habits increased not in quantity but in quality. It seemed more revelation knowledge came to me as I read the Word of God, and the Bible came alive. But it should be noted that this didn't happen overnight; it was a process—one I'm still undergoing as I continue this practice.

From experience, I don't personally understand how anyone could not want to practice speaking and praying in tongues on a regular basis. In fact, I felt like all those years I was saved without the baptism of the Holy Spirit I was missing out. Now I can't even imagine how to pray without this gift because it has become so integrated into my prayer habits. It is unfortunate that disagreement exists in the body of Christ over this issue, but it's the person who lacks the experience who is without foundation for his or her argument, because Scripture sufficiently instructs and explains this subject quite clearly.

The devil knows what a threat a believer, who can tap into this revelation knowledge and edification process through a personal tutor like the Holy Spirit, is to the kingdom of darkness. It makes sense then that the devil would attempt to confuse its use and get believers to dispute it and avoid it by relegating its use only to a certain time era instead of the present. Or better yet, that he would demonize its use and cause believers to believe those who practice it are the ones engaging in strange fire.

Once a clear case is made and all objections to its use are cleared out of the skeptic's mind, then the instructions on the use of the gift of tongues and the purpose behind the tongues for edification are both evident and clear. It really is one of the most enjoyable and spiritual acts the believer can do. Praying in tongues is about as supernatural as raising the dead since both have nothing to do with us but with God. With that kind of power working within us, which is accessible by praying in the Spirit, who wouldn't want to pray in tongues?

Notes

1. Dave Roberson, *The Walk of the Spirit, The Walk of Power*, 211, 215.

2. Ibid., 16.

3. Ibid., 129.

4. "Releasing the Power of the Holy Spirit" by Dave Roberson, *Fresh Outlook Magazine*, Sept/Oct 2005, http://freshoutlookmag.com/articles/SeptOct05-article2.html (accessed on November 1, 2013).

Chapter 15

The Holy Spirit Brings Us into All Truth

*I*n John 17 Jesus said that the Holy Spirit would teach us *all* things. The disciples, who were the ones being spoken to here, didn't have all of Jesus's words written down in a Bible yet for the Holy Spirit to bring revelation from. Jesus was not telling them the Holy Spirit would help them memorize the Romans Road or the Sermon on the Mount. They had to rely on the Holy Spirit to bring to remembrance what he had *personally told them*. They would not be relying on mental or spiritual recollection of the Bible as a literary text. Rather, they had the Word himself—Jesus Christ—in their midst for three and a half years to personally learn from. However, since believers today do not have that exact experience as they did, it's not a misinterpretation to take this text to say that the Holy Spirit brings life to the *written* Word for us this way two thousand years later.

The very first few verses of the book of Genesis mention how the Spirit of the Lord was hovering over the face of the waters (Genesis 1:2). He was involved when God *spoke* the Word and brought forth life in the midst of chaos, including God breathing life into the dust, thus creating the first man. The Psalms mention how God knew us before he formed us in the womb (Psalm 139:13-16). Before we ever set foot on the face of the earth and began to speak some goo-goos and gah-gahs, the Lord had a plan for each of our individual lives. And it is this that the Holy Spirit brings to remembrance in us as we pray in tongues.

> **The Holy Spirit is never going to contradict what he has allowed to be written down in the Bible.**

The Holy Spirit—who is living in you if you're a believer—repeats to you and gives you revelation and insight into the things God has spoken and decreed about your life before the foundation of the world. He helps build you up and qualify you *into* that plan that is God's will for your life. God has a "perfect" will for us that is possible to miss. He has set up in his unending and unfathomable wisdom a way to deposit that will on the inside of us, and then let us unpack it at our own pace through praying in tongues—edifying ourselves in the spirit, and growing in our faith as a result. We can't pray consistently in tongues for very long before the things that don't belong in God's plan for us begin to fall away. Through this process, the Holy Spirit is able to build into our hearts the understanding of God's perfect will for our lives.

In that same chapter of John's Gospel (17), Jesus was not exclusively talking only about the words he spoke at that time (which was over two thousand years ago). Rather, the Holy Spirit is capable of remembering words that have been spoken no matter how long ago they were spoken. He is not bound by time and space like we are. Everything that has ever happened or will ever happen has already happened and not yet happened, in a manner of speaking, from his point of view. The moment that he was hovering over the waters in Genesis 1:2 and the moment he speaks of in Revelation 22:17, inviting the Lord Jesus to come back, are on the same level in the history of existence in God's sight. This stuff is hard for us finite-thinking beings to understand since we're linear and bound by time. According to Jesus, however, the Spirit of God takes the things he has heard about your life and the plan God has for it and reveals them to you.

When and where exactly did the Holy Ghost *hear* the things that he tells us? Well, friend, did you know this includes things that are not "written in the Book"? This includes the calling God has for you—your purpose and your destiny. This includes whom you'll marry and even what you should do today. However, the Holy Spirit is never going to contradict what he has allowed to be written down in the Bible. The Author of that Book is never going to give you revelation that contradicts the Book that he penned through human hands. Remember, the Spirit and the Word are one (1 John 5:7). If you ever hear someone giving some "new teaching" that they say God revealed to them, ask them for at least three Scripture passages to back it up.

Abiding in Christ

"Steve, what on earth does this revelation stuff and speaking in tongues have to do with interpretations?" Well, I'm glad you asked. I'm saying all this to say that extended times of praying in tongues are directly related to personal edification and revelation and inner fortification. I've moved from dismantling theological barriers and misunderstandings about speaking in tongues to hopefully getting you jealous to be doing it more in your life—if you're not already—and realize the benefits to your spiritual growth that this exercise produces in you.

Slowly or speedily, the level of your spiritual growth is completely up to you—in the same way an athlete decides how much time he's going to spend in the gym working out and developing his muscles. God doesn't sovereignly "ordain" him to just get fit and develop bulging biceps overnight. The athlete is in charge of how much he is going to do this practice, and likewise every believer is a steward of his or her own spiritual edification. Speaking and praying in the Holy Spirit is a tremendous aid in watering the seed of our faith and in helping us strengthen our roots as they go deeper in him.

One of the most profound ways I have been impacted about the role speaking and praying in tongues has in our lives with relation to growth and overcoming sin is found in a passage that's not even about the spiritual gifts. Instead, it comes from the passage that, for me, is the quintessential book on the love of God: the Song of Solomon.

I'm currently working on a project about the Song, which, like aged wine, probably won't be ready for another few years at the earliest. I mention this here because I feel it's necessary to establish a bit of groundwork for this passage before using it to teach a principle about praying in tongues.

> *O my dove, in the clefts of the rock, in the crannies of the cliff, let me see your face, let me hear your voice, for your voice is sweet, and your face is lovely. Catch*

the foxes for us, the little foxes that spoil the vine-yards, for our vineyards are in blossom. (Song of Solomon 2:14-15)

The whole book, whether you read it allegorically or just as a song, is about the love between a bridegroom and his bride. We can glean from it in more specific and personal ways for our individual journeys with the Lord, and not just the collective body of Christ. When I read these simple yet profound verses in the Song, I'm compelled to think of passages like the following in the Gospel of John:

I am the true vine, and my Father is the vinedresser. Every branch of mine that does not bear fruit He takes away, and every branch that does bear fruit He prunes, that it may bear more fruit. Already you are clean because of the word that I have spoken to you. Abide in Me, and I in you. As the branch cannot bear fruit by itself, unless it abides in the vine, neither can you unless you abide in Me. I am the vine; you are the branches. Whoever abides in Me and I in him, he it is that bears much fruit, for apart from Me you can do nothing. (John 15:1-5, NKJV)

When we spend time abiding in Christ and cultivating intimacy with him, we go to the "hiding place," which signifies a place of privacy. It speaks of letting him hear our voice, hence reinforcing that we shouldn't *only* think our prayers, but God actually desires to hear it come out of our mouths as well. Hearing our voice is also applied to our worship of him too.

The Hebrew word for *ruin* in Song of Solomon 2:15 is *châbal*. Its primitive root means to wind tightly as a rope, or to bind, specifically by a pledge. It also figuratively means to pervert, destroy, or to writhe in pain, especially of parturition. The English Standard Version I quoted from above uses the word *spoil*, which shows the same concept.

The foxes represent the devil or his demons, and they could also be applied to our flesh and our carnal leanings, as well as other tendencies or earthly distractions. In our neglect of our relationship with Christ, the opportunity is created for outside spiritual and demonic schemes to come into our lives. In either case, if the foxes are not dealt with at this time, they will cause more damage and be much more difficult to overcome as time goes on.[1]

When we're growing and the vineyard is in bloom and ripe, *that* is the time the fruit is the most vulnerable and sensitive. Little foxes can destroy the vine that yields fruit. They do this by gnawing and breaking the little branches, leaves, and the bark by digging holes in the vineyards, and so *spoiling the roots* by eating the grapes and hindering the growth of the vine.

> The devil is always seeking to destroy us in any way he possibly can. There's no better way to do it than at the foundational root level, like the foxes seek to do in the vineyard.

Our Firstfruits

Vineyards are cultivated for producing grapes, which are then used to produce wine. Galatians 5:22-23 lists the fruit of the

Spirit, which are some of the evidences there will be in our lives if we're intimately connected to the vine. We'll produce fruit and become more like him in whom we're beholding and whose image we're being transformed into.

Though different symbols are used in different ways throughout Scripture, the vineyard is often a type or a symbol of the church in the New Testament, Israel in the Old Testament, and the people of God in general. Wine is correlated with the work of the Holy Spirit, and it is used in Solomon's Song 1:2 and 4:10 as representative of the good things and finer pleasures of this world.

The devil is always seeking to destroy us in any way he possibly can. He desires to ruin the work of the Spirit in our lives individually and collectively as the body of Christ. There's no better way to do it than at the foundational root level, like the foxes seek to do in the vineyard.

We know one symbol for the Holy Spirit is *new* wine, which is made from fresh, just-picked grapes. The passage here in the Song of Solomon talks about how the foxes ruin the vineyards that are in bloom—when they're young, tender, and sensitive. Most plants and trees require that you remove the firstfruits as soon as they appear, and then after that the fruit will appear in larger size and in more quantity. However, if it's not obtained properly in that firstfruit stage, the tree will never grow properly and yield very much fruit—in other words, it *will never realize its full potential.*

I'm sure there's a sermon in there on giving God our firstfruits with all things in our lives, but that's another book. Suffice it to say here that it's the *first*fruits the foxes are trying to spoil in order to prevent the vine from ever reaching its full potential. Therefore, it is at this crucial moment the foxes must be stopped from doing any damage or else it will be irreparable, and the young one in Christ may not fully recover from the damage caused.

Intimacy with God

God calls us through this passage to the hiding place in the rock (the Rock Christ Jesus) and wants to see our face and hear our voice. This is of course indicative of prayer, definitely indicating *intimacy* with God. Viewing these verses through that lens, we see that if we go up into God and be alone with him through intimate praying that we will wind up "catching those foxes" that ruin the Spirit's work in our lives because we're bound to them instead of walking in our freedom.

When the vineyard is getting watered with the Word of God (Ephesians 5:26), then the things of the Spirit will flow, such as the gifts, the fruit, and new wine revelation. It's *this* the foxes are trying to destroy, stop, pervert, or prevent from happening. But Paul writes that we are to fix our gaze upon the Lord, thus being changed more and more into his image:

> *Now the Lord is the Spirit, and where the Spirit of the Lord is, there is freedom. And we all, with unveiled face, beholding the glory of the Lord, are being transformed into the same image from one degree of glory to another. For this comes from the Lord who is the Spirit.* (2 Corinthians 3:17-18)

If you are struggling with fleshly tendencies, or in overcoming habitual sin, my personal experience and understanding of this passage causes me to encourage you to go be alone with

Christ and "behold him" in this manner. Doing so will help you catch the foxes in your life that spoil the work of the Holy Spirit, and the Spirit in turn will help you grow strong in your inner spirit to overcome these areas and be transformed more and more into the image of Christ. Like the bridegroom here who is inviting his bride to come be alone with him, we know that God invites us to draw near to him and he will draw near to us (James 4:8).

> Be intimate with Christ, and pray a whole lot in tongues as well. Not only will it help with your understanding and revelation of the Word of God, but it will also help crucify your flesh and overcome the foxes that are holding you back.

Inoculation against Deception

Notice how it states in the Song of Solomon 2:14 that he loves the sound of her voice. So what better thing to be offering up with our voices than tongues, since according to Romans 8:26 we don't know what we ought to be praying for as we ought? Jude 20 mentions that praying in the Holy Spirit is to build ourselves up on our most holy faith. Another way of saying it is that praying in tongues builds up the inner spirit and helps keep those foxes from spoiling the vine.

Jude was writing to the early church—which was young and still in formation like "tender grapes"—to contend for the faith because false doctrine (foxes) had gotten into the church and was rendering it powerless at this crucial moment in history. Early on, while the body of Christ was still young and getting established, much like the vineyard with grapes in bloom during springtime, it was the most sensitive and important time for false doctrine to be weeded out. The remedy to that is found in verse 20, which suggests we are to pray in the Holy Ghost. Praying in the Spirit is our inoculation against false doctrine (the foxes) because it is how the Holy Spirit teaches us.

The apostle John stated something very similar to this in his epistle:

> *I write these things to you about those who are trying to deceive you. But the anointing* (of the Holy Spirit) *that you received from him abides in you, and you have no need that anyone should teach you. But as his anointing teaches you about everything, and is true, and is no lie—just as it has taught you, abide in him.* (1 John 2:26-27)

Abiding in the Holy Spirit is the way you'll avoid and be protected from deception.

Be intimate with Christ, and pray a whole lot in tongues as well. Not only will it help with your understanding and revelation of the Word of God, but it will also help crucify your flesh and overcome the foxes that are holding you back. As you dwell in the pure Word of God and allow it to water your vineyard, it will result in the wine of the Holy Spirit being produced and flowing in your life since he is more easily able to flow through those who are intimate with Christ and full of the Word of God.

Note

1. The reader is encouraged to read more about this in my e-book *The Imperishable Seed of Christ* for further elaboration that we won't go into here for brevity's sake.

Chapter 16

Love: The More Excellent Way

How much better is your love than wine, and
the fragrance of your oils than any spice!
—SONG OF SOLOMON 4:10

And I will show you a still more excellent way.
—1 CORINTHIANS 12:31

In the opening of the Song of Solomon—my favorite book in the Old Testament, if not the whole Bible—the Shulamite shepherdess states of her lover that his love is better than wine (Song of Solomon 1:2). Then midway through the song when he speaks of what fascinates him about *her*, we're told the same thing (Song of Solomon 4:10). The song is to be interpreted as a representation of the Bridegroom's love toward the church, his bride. We know that Jesus is better than anything in this world, and the obvious interpretation of that phrase would lead the believer to say, "Of course he is!"

Therefore, if he is saying of her that *her* love is better than wine, then we can automatically rule out that he would be saying her love is better than *any* sin since he lived a sin*less* life and died to save us from our sins. He would not have engaged in any carnal pleasure that he'd compare her love with. No, she finds his love to be even better than the *good* pleasure this life has to offer, even things that aren't inherently sinful or wrong. Likewise, he finds her affection and devotion to him better than wine. The Lord finds our love toward him to be more intoxicating than wine. Scripture says God desires obedience and loyalty more than sacrifice (Hosea 6:6). If you would get a revelation that you are the apple of God's eye, and that the love you express in response to his love blows him away, I'm convinced it would change and sustain you in deeper ways than you've ever imagined.

What is the significance of this, and how does this relate to speaking in tongues?

> The operation of spiritual gifts is to be *the norm* for the contemporary church, and that they are exactly what a gift is supposed to be—something given to us freely without our earning it.

The Love of God as a Motivation for Operating in the Spiritual Gifts

*Now there are varieties of gifts, but the same Spirit.... To each is given **the manifestation of the Spirit** for the common good.* (1 Corinthians 12:4, 7)

Jesus will use the Holy Spirit to bring us to maturity in the love walk. Oftentimes, in the Old Testament, wine is used symbolically to represent the Holy Spirit. The often quoted Ephesians 5:17-21 is not saying the Holy Spirit is wine or that being filled with him is like being drunk with wine; instead, Paul is suggesting that when we're filled with the Spirit we won't act drunk, but we'll do the things listed, such as "addressing one another in psalms and hymns and spiritual songs, singing and making melody to the Lord with your heart, giving thanks always and for everything to God the Father in the name of our Lord Jesus Christ, submitting to one another out of reverence for Christ."

In First Corinthians 12, Paul goes into significant detail about the gifts of the Holy Spirit and their operation in the context of the church. Hopefully I've done a decent job explaining why I am convinced the operation of spiritual gifts is to be *the norm* for the contemporary church, and that they are exactly what a gift is supposed to be—something given to us freely without our earning it. At the same time, if tongues are foundational or basic to the life of the church, then that means they're not the epitome of spiritual maturity, but only a starting point. Paul states at the end of 1 Corinthians 12, "I will show you a still more excellent way" (1 Corinthians 12:31). A more excellent way than *what*?

The answer to that question is found in verse 11: "All these (gifts) are *empowered* by one and the same Spirit, who *apportions to each* one individually *as he wills*." Most in the church emphasize chapters 12 and 14 but skip chapter 13, which is commonly called the "love chapter." Then still others, fearing misuse of the spiritual enablements, overemphasize the love chapter to the exclusion of the other two chapters that sandwich it. Both love and the gifts are necessary in community with other Christians. Paul said:

> If I speak in the tongues of men and of angels, **but have not love**, I am a noisy gong or a clanging cymbal. And if I have prophetic powers, and understand all mysteries and all knowledge, and if I have all faith, so as to remove mountains, **but have not love, I am nothing**. (1 Corinthians 13:1-2)

When I learned Spanish, I started with basic concepts. As I matured in my understanding and use of the language, however, I still needed the basic concepts I learned at the beginning. I didn't do away with them now that I had advanced and spoke Spanish with more fluency. Moving on to more advanced understanding has not meant that I no longer needed the basic aspects of this language. The seemingly lesser (basic) Spanish provided a foundation for the other things I'd go on to learn in mastering the language. Likewise, the lesser or more basic spiritual enablements are included in the greater, but they are not diminished by it.

The lesser, in this case, is that the gifts are distributed as the Spirit wills, and the greater work is love. But I repeat, the greater doesn't nullify or do away with the lesser. It is out of love that you will most effectively minister in the spiritual gifts. Maturing into love doesn't mean you no longer need the gifts; on the contrary, Paul didn't say, "*Instead* I will show you a more excellent way," but he said "and." This changes our traditional understanding profoundly. The two go together, and the fact that Paul goes into talking about love is building on the foundation (of the basic use of the gifts), not replacing it. This is why he goes on to write:

When I was a child, I spoke like a child, I thought like a child, I reasoned like a child. **When I became a man, I gave up childish ways.** *For now we see in a mirror dimly, but then face to face. Now I know in part; then I shall know fully, even as I have been fully known.* (1 Corinthians 13:11-12)

> **The gifts of the Spirit are not the "be all and end all" or the telltale sign of spiritual maturity, but rather the opposite: they're just a beginning, or a foundation, and we're to move on in maturity from there.**

When we are children in the Lord, it is necessary for the Holy Spirit to distribute the gifts in our lives and in the members of the body of Christ as he sees fit. When children are little, there is more supervision needed in their lives, even of some good and "safe" gifts they've been given. Maybe, for example, a daughter has received a laptop computer or tablet, and she has Internet access. The child may have this particular technological gift, but her parents will still put limitations on it, such as time allowed, and maybe even filter what sites she visits. But as time goes on and the child matures (hopefully!), she will become more self-disciplined and know how to manage her time well, learning to be more discerning as an adult. As she matures, she proves to be faithful with what she has been entrusted with. Gradually she will need less and less supervision.

Maybe one day the child will become an Internet marketer, fully aware of how to use her computer for profitable purposes with her own skills and talents, and she no longer uses it just to play video games or chat with friends. She may wind up donating a large portion of her profits to those in need in other places in the world. When she hears of problems people are going through, she may write e-mails to encourage them. Now mature and motivated by love, she knows *how* to do things without being instructed or given suggestions by her parents. Her relationship with her parents has not changed at all. In the fact, she is still their daughter and they are still her parents, but they have changed her childish ways and *no longer needs the same type of involvement* or monitoring of her online activity. Now that she has grown up, her relationship with her parents reflects a more mature nature. She can be depended on to make right decisions because she is no longer a five-year-old child.

I realize this example is far from perfect, but I wish to draw the point that the gifts of the Spirit are basic at the fundamental and foundational level of our Christian lives. They are not the "be all and end all" or the telltale sign of spiritual maturity, but rather the opposite: they're just a beginning, or a foundation, and we're to move on in maturity from there. We build on that foundation. The entire book of 1 Corinthians shows that flawed, imperfect, and even selfish people still operate in the things the Spirit has enabled them to, but this does not signify that they are mature or walking in love toward one another. As we have already mentioned, nothing in the book of First Corinthians is deep or profound, as Paul said he was giving them milk and they were not yet ready for meat (1 Corinthians 3:2).

The shepherdess in the Song of Solomon says his (Christ's) love is more excellent than wine, which represents the good and noble things in life, which may even be referring to things inspired by the Holy Spirit. If you are being filled with the Holy

Spirit—as our familiar passage in Ephesians 5 says—you won't only be speaking and making melody in your heart, but you will also be "submitting to one another out of reverence for Christ" (Ephesians 5:21). What is submission other than merely preferring the other person more than yourself out of the *agape* love poured out in your heart as you continually receive the infilling of the wine of the Holy Spirit? Now "your love is better than wine" and "I will show you a more excellent way" both have more significant and impacting meaning to me than they did before.

> **The real evidence of being filled with the Holy Spirit is love for one another; not at the expense of the gifts, such as tongues, but on top of it, including the gifts.**

There is no reason for a Christ follower not to speak in tongues. You may wish not to or choose to continue believing it's not necessary, but I don't look to speaking in tongues as the primary evidence of someone being filled with the Holy Spirit. At some point, we should move on from doing this as a basic foundation and on to other things. Babies begin by making noises and forming syllables, and they eventually grow to carry on real conversations and, hopefully by the time they're adults, no longer think the world revolves around them.

Do you love? One of the real evidences of a born-again believer truly being filled with the Holy Spirit is going to be *love*, but with speaking in tongues thrown in too. It's like buying a car. The car is powered by love but the noise the engine makes is tongues. If we are operating in all manner of gifts of the Spirit, but have not love, then it is pointless and we are nothing (1 Cor-inthians 13:1-2). If the car makes noise but doesn't move, then it's all for nothing. If we are constantly and regularly being filled with the Holy Spirit on an ongoing basis, then it won't just be evidenced by speaking in tongues, prophecies, psalms, hymns, and so on, but we will also be submitting to one another out of reverence for Christ.

Dare I say it this way: the *real* evidence of being filled with the Holy Spirit is love for one another, but not at the expense of the gifts, such as tongues, but on top of it, including the gifts. How do I know this? John writes:

> We love because he first loved us. If anyone says, "I love God," and hates his brother, he is a liar; for he who does not love his brother whom he has seen cannot love God whom he has not seen. And this commandment we have from him: whoever loves God must also love his brother. (1 John 4:19-20)

You can sheebie deeby and shaka boom like the rest of them and then turn around and gossip about your brother in Christ. John, the man who self-identified as "the disciple Jesus loved" all throughout his Gospel had some very serious things to say about love in his epistle toward the end of the New Testament about not walking in love.

We must remember a few things about the apostle John—he had a revelation of the love of God which obviously would affect his perspective. In the end of his Gospel, he said that if all the works Jesus did were recorded, the world would not be able to contain the books (John 21:25). Therefore, what we have written in our Scripture canon does not contain any wasted pages. All of it is divinely arranged to be there for a particular reason. John lived to a ripe old age and it's commonly held by many that he wrote this and his other two epistles toward the very end of his life, even after he wrote the Revelation he received while exiled on the island of Patmos.

If John took the time to write these five chapters after decades of ministry, then the stuff he wrote *must* be some of the most important things he felt worth sharing with the recipient of this letter and the church. Therefore, it's wise of us to take his words seriously and meditate upon and ponder things from the perspective he would have been writing from. We need the perspective of the one who knew his identity in the bride of Christ.

> **Our ability to speak in tongues, though we have it, means nothing if we're not submitting to one another out of love and preferring one another's needs above our own.**

How do I know this whole "wine of the Spirit" and "being filled, speaking to one another, and submitting to one another" thing ties into the whole bridal paradigm? Because the rest of Ephesians 5 goes on to say so:

> *Wives, submit to your own husbands, as to the Lord. For the husband is the head of the wife even as Christ is the head of the church, his body, and is himself its Savior. Now as the church submits to Christ, so also wives should submit in everything to their husbands.* (Ephesians 5:22-24)

Sometimes I really hate the chapter breaks and title headers the publishers of our Bible translations put in there, because the original manuscripts were not broken down into chapters and verses, and they certainly didn't have subject headings like most of our Bibles do today. I'm only mentioning this pet peeve of mine because even though they're helpful for finding specific passages and parables, when reading they sometimes inadvertently give the reader the impression new topics are starting. However, this is a part of the same flow of thought the author had. Paul goes on further to say:

> In the same way husbands should love their wives as their own bodies. He who loves his wife loves himself. For no one ever hated his own flesh, but nourishes and cherishes it, just as Christ does the church, because we are members of his body. (Ephesians 5:28-30)

If we have truly been born from above, and filled with the Holy Spirit, we're going to respect Christ's bride—the church and the members thereof—the way the wife is to respect her husband. If we respect Christ out of the response we have toward him as he loves us, then we will not do anything to hurt his bride that we're a part of. We will lay our life down for one another. We will speak encouragement to each other, not gossip. We will submit to one another, preferring the other as better than ourselves. Our ability to speak in tongues, though we have it, means nothing if we're not submitting to one another out of love and preferring one another's needs above our own. It's just the beginning. When we submit to one another out of reverence for Christ, he finds that to be better than wine.

Paul finished the love chapter by writing, "So now faith, hope, and love abide, these three; but the greatest of these is love" (1 Corinthians 13:13). This is the more excellent way. Speak in tongues a lot, but don't stop there! It's just the beginning of the love walk.

Prayer to Receive the Baptism in the Holy Spirit

irst, let me say there's not a specific template you should follow for how to receive the baptism in the Holy Spirit. I doubt if you say the words wrong, it won't happen or God will withhold it from you. God hears the cry of your heart and answers those who seek him, so it's not so much about the words you pray but the fact you're asking God to fill you with his Spirit, which he is more than delighted to do.

I've prayed with friends using text messaging by typing out prayers to pray on their end and they have received the baptism in the Holy Spirit. I've known others who woke up from sleeping and immediately were baptized and speaking in tongues. I've prayed with others over the phone, Skype, and through other technologies. I generally prefer laying hands on people and encouraging them when I pray for them; however, there are no limitations to how the Holy Spirit can give you this gift. Not to mention, it really is a simple matter to receive this precious gift from the Lord.

Pray with me today:

> *Dear Heavenly Father,*
>
> *Your Word says that you are faithful to give the Holy Spirit to those who ask you. So in the name of Jesus, I ask you to please fill me with the Holy Spirit. I thank you for giving me a new language along with this filling. I believe I receive it right now. Thank you for this wonderful gift. Amen.*

Now as the new syllables start rising up from inside your inner spirit, you'll be tempted to ignore them and expect something more spectacular to happen. But it really is that simple. If you're praying this prayer by yourself, you've got the added benefit of not being tempted to merely repeat what someone else is saying or praying. You can tune into that place in your inner spirit where the Holy Ghost is bringing the new language from and simply yield to it. Begin to speak out these words that you don't understand with your mind but you know the Holy Spirit is birthing in you.

You may sound silly. Actually, I guarantee that you will sound silly. You'll sound a lot like a baby in the beginning. The more you continue to speak these words, the more they will flow out of your spirit. It will become more natural to you and you'll find yourself becoming more and more fluent in your new prayer language. I encourage you to spend several minutes speaking in this new language so you can see for yourself not only how easy it is but how natural it is as well.

Now pray in the Holy Spirit much and often. Your life will never be the same again.

How to Lead Someone in the Baptism in the Holy Spirit

*T*he following is a handout my friend and FIRE School of Ministry teacher Brian Parkman gives to students in his classes on the Holy Spirit. If you are not yet baptized in the Holy Spirit, or you believe you are but have not yet spoken in tongues, this will also help instruct you in how to receive the baptism in the Holy Spirit.

I've made changes so as to make it flow differently for a book format. There is some repetition here from previous chapters but that's so you can use this section of the book if you want to access it on your phone or mobile device when ministering the baptism in the Holy Spirit to an individual.

Faith begins where the will of God is known. The purpose of ministering in this way is so that a person's faith will be built by a proper foundation from Scripture on God's will concerning the infilling of the Holy Spirit. Before you can get a person to receive, you have to get them to hear what God's Word says about the baptism in the Spirit, then they'll know two things: what they can expect from God and what God expects of them.

I also attempt to get them to disregard everything they have heard or been taught up to this point about receiving the baptism in the Holy Spirit. If what they had heard or been taught was correct, then they wouldn't be having me pray for them at this point in time.

It is important to get them to understand that they're not asking God to give them the Holy Spirit. They are praying to receive him. The Holy Spirit was sent on the day of Pentecost. God did not yank him back up into heaven after that day only to pour him out again repeatedly on people who beg him. God has already given him. You are simply teaching them how to receive. They don't have to beg. As a matter of fact, if they start begging, then they are putting the responsibility off on God. But he has already given. Again, it is up to them to receive what has already been given. I will use the example of someone handing them a glass of water. They take the water and they drink. Being filled with the Holy Spirit is as easy as taking a drink of water when thirsty.

Another thing, and this may seem quite obvious, but make sure they are saved. There have been times I have just assumed that was so, and it turned out not to be. Ask them. If you are ministering to a group of people, do the same thing with the entire group.

Tell them they are not seeking tongues here; they are going to be filled with the Spirit. Tongues are just an evidence of the power they are going to receive through the filling of the Holy Spirit. When I start a car, I can hear the engine running, but that sound is not what I am after—it is just evidence that the power is active, that the engine is running.

When you are attempting to get people to receive you must always overcome every objection, correct every error, and remove every stumbling block. Why? Because people have many misconceptions and wrong teachings concerning the baptism in the Holy Spirit. If they have been seeking the baptism for a while, this is obvious or they would have already been filled.

The three main stumbling blocks that I have found that keep people from receiving are:

1. Not believing in the baptism in the Holy Spirit (unbelief).

2. Thinking that the Holy Spirit is going to take them over, control them, make them speak, or talk through them (error).

3. Expecting a spectacular supernatural experience (stumbling block).

Since I know that these are areas where they have the most problems, I cover these issues when ministering to them before praying with them. The Scriptures in Acts are used to make clear to them that in each instance when they were filled with the Holy Spirit that they spoke with tongues.

In Acts 2:1-4 everyone gathered there were *all* filled and began to *speak with other tongues.* Emphasize all and that they will speak with tongues also. They were all filled and began to speak. Who spoke? *They* began to speak, not the Holy Spirit. The Spirit gave them utterance or unction. It is the Spirit that gives the utterance or unction, but it is the individual who speaks. The Holy Spirit does not speak with tongues—*you* do. Reference 1 Corinthians 14:14: "For if I pray in an unknown tongue, my spirit prayeth..." (KJV). *My* spirit prays, not the Holy Spirit.

At this point use this illustration to help them understand how they are to speak and yield to the Holy Spirit. A lot of people think that the Holy Spirit comes in and takes them over and makes them speak or talks through them. He does not do the speaking; he just gives them the unction or inspiration to speak. He prompts them to speak, but doesn't do it for them. The individual is the one who speaks.

It is not like someone took a small radio and turned it on, and turned the volume up all the way, and you swallowed it, and you just opened up your mouth and it played out of you. No. *You* have to do the speaking. You have to use *your own* vocal chords, your own tongue, your own air, and your own mouth, and speak just like you do when you talk in your native language. However, instead of speaking the language you know, you speak what he prompts or inspires you to speak. You do the speaking even though he gives the unction, utterance, or inspiration.

I might also use this illustration if I know they have been saved awhile and ask them: have you ever been talking to someone about the Lord and the Holy Spirit began to inspire you what to say? You thought to yourself, "That wasn't me. Things just began coming out of my mouth that I hadn't even thought of saying before that point." The Holy Spirit inspired you, but he didn't talk for you. You did the talking. He gave you the inspiration. That is the way the baptism in the Holy Spirit works.

In Acts 10:44-46 we read about how the Holy Spirit fell on those who *heard the Word*, then they heard them *speak with tongues*. Give them the background of the story about Cornelius sending for Peter. Tell them they are hearing the Word and when you pray for them they will speak in tongues also.

In Acts 19:1-6 Paul laid hands on some of the disciples of John. The Holy Spirit came on them and they spoke with tongues. Again, you are just letting them see that when the Holy Spirit came on John's disciples they spoke in tongues. Tell them, "When I lay hands on you the Holy Spirit will come on you and you will speak in tongues also."

Then in Luke 11:9-13 Jesus said that if we ask it will be given. If we, being capable of evil, will give our children what they ask for, how much more will our heavenly Father give us the Holy Spirit if we ask him? You will get what you ask for. You will not get an evil spirit, but the Holy Spirit.

Then deal with the stumbling block of expecting a spectacular supernatural experience to occur. Tell them, "That is the exception and not the rule." Use Paul getting saved as an example. It was a very spectacular conversion experience. But the way he was saved was an exception, not the rule of how it happens for every individual. If someone else was waiting on an experience like his to get saved, they might never be saved. Tell them they probably won't feel anything at all. Set them up to receive by faith, not their feelings. If they do get feelings, then that is just gravy.

Then I go through this scenario: "When I lay hands on you and tell you to receive the Holy Spirit, as an act of faith, close your eyes, open your mouth, take a deep breath, and in your mind see the Holy Spirit coming in and filling you. When you breathe out, just begin to speak what the Holy Spirit is giving you."

Then have them repeat a prayer after you asking for Jesus to fill them with the Holy Spirit. At the end of this prayer have them repeat, "When hands are laid on me, I will speak in tongues." Then tell them to receive the Holy Spirit and lay hands on them. They should raise their hands as you instructed them and breathe in, and they should begin speaking in tongues.

As you lay hands on them and tell them to receive, begin to pray in tongues yourself as they are receiving. You may have to encourage them somewhat during this time. Sometimes they will begin to pray in English (or whatever their native language is), so you have to encourage them to not speak in English as they cannot speak two languages at the same time. Tell them to say nothing but what the Spirit is inspiring them to say.

Once they receive, then I minister to the immediate concerns they might have. The most frequent one is thinking "it was just me" who was speaking in tongues. After they have prayed in tongues for a little while (let them pray for more than a few minutes and pray in tongues along with them) and have stopped, I will say something like this: "Now the first thing you are going to think is that 'that was just me.' Well, it was you. Remember what we saw in Acts 2? It said 'they,' meaning the ones in the upper room began to speak in tongues. But the Spirit gave the utterance or inspiration. So it was you speaking in tongues, but it was the Holy Spirit inspiring you what to say. First Corinthians 14:14 says, 'For if I pray in an unknown tongue, my spirit prays.' So it is your spirit doing the praying, not the Holy Spirit."

As you gain experience, you will be able to judge each situation separately, and you may not go through everything that I have put in this document. The most important part is covering error number two and using the illustration concerning the radio mentioned earlier. This is the greatest hindrance—thinking the Holy Spirit is going to come on them and control them and make them speak, as opposed to them having to yield to the Holy Spirit and them doing the actual speaking. In most of the people I have ministered to, this is the main reason they have not received.

Another thing I will do after having dealt with them thinking it was "just them" is to have them pray in tongues again as I pray along with them. This is just to make them more comfortable with their prayer language and to show them they can now yield to their prayer language any time they want. Paul said in First Corinthians 14:15, "I will pray with my spirit, but I will pray with my mind also." In other words, it is an act of their will to yield to the Holy Spirit any time they want.

About Steve Bremner

*S*teve Bremner is a missionary to Peru and a FIRE School of Ministry graduate. He has a burden for grounding people in the Word of God and seeing believers from all sorts of backgrounds live out and experience the power of the Holy Spirit and the love of God in their lives and ministries.

Steve also thinks it's pretentious when authors write their own bio pages but refer to themselves in the third person. I—I mean *he*—served in the Netherlands for almost two years before moving to South America. The gift of teaching and a pastoral heart are what characterize Steve's calling, and in Peru he's had opportunities to teach in a local seminary, share the love of Christ to some of the underprivileged, and traveled to shanty towns outside of Lima, the nation's capital, to teach with and serve alongside other established ministries. He is now living in Chorrillos, and is part of a missional community called Oikos, where he teaches full time in its school of ministry.

Steve is Canadian (and is not ashamed of it), and was sent out by River Run Fellowship, located in Peterborough, Ontario. That's in Canada, for those who need it clarified. If it weren't for his home fellowship, and its lead elder Stephen Best, he would never have gone to Peru where he is beginning to see God do things he once only imagined and daydreamed about.

Like any other authors, Steve and Lili Bremner are using the proceeds from their book sales to finance their disciple making in Peru. Your purchase of this book is greatly appreciated, and you are invited to purchase his other titles if you enjoyed this book. One way you can support him that doesn't require any of your money is by writing a review of this book in the online store you bought it in and recommending it to others.

Fire on Your Head Podcast

*I*f the Internet had been available to the apostle Paul, he'd have used it make the Word of God available to as many people as he possibly could. For this reason, Steve cohosts and produces the *Fire On Your Head* podcast, with other contributors to *Fire Press*—an online Christian magazine he founded in 2008, and currently serves as senior editor, and where he has spent years sharpening his writing skills.

The *Fire On Your Head* podcast can be subscribed to in iTunes and other popular pod catcher programs such as Stitcher Radio, or you can visit the site directly at www.fireonyourhead .com.

Connect with Us

To be notified when Steve's other projects are released, follow him on social media at the following links:

Facebook.com/StephenGeorgeBremner

Twitter.com/StephenGBremner

plus.google.com/+SteveBremner

Or you can join Steve and Lili's ministry e-mail list and receive other stuff, such as newsletters and updates from his website at www.SteveBremner.com.

Partner with Us

*I*f you were touched by this book and would like to make a donation to sow directly into Steve and Lili Bremner on the mission field in Peru, please follow these instructions:

In Canada make checks payable to:

CALVARY INTERNATIONAL CANADA
149 Westmount Dr. N, P.O. Box 20081,
Orillia, Ontario L3V 6C7

Please write "805C" in the memo line. Do *not* write Steve or missionary anywhere on the check because it will not be received. Visit their site to donate online at http://calvaryintcanada.com/, or go specifically to http://calvaryintcanada.com/805c/ if you'd like to set up recurring monthly donations for Steve and Lili.

In the USA make checks payable to:

WORLD OUTREACH CENTER
PO Box 3478,
Fort Mill, SC 29708

Please indicate that it is for the Bremners/Peru.

If you would like to donate online, then please visit www.worldoutreachcommunity.org.

Thank you for your encouragement and support.